COUNTRY ADVENTURES

IN MARYLAND, VIRGINIA & WEST VIRGINIA

BY JOAN MOONEY

A revision of the original work by Elizabeth C. Mooney

Published by
The Washington Book Trading Company, Arlington, Virginia

Book Design: Ed Schneider
Editor: Raissa M. Modrak
Type: Gerryamanda, Washington, D.C.
Printing: by Balmar Printing, Gaithersburg, Maryland
Published by WBT: The Washington Book Trading Company
P.O. Box 1676, Arlington, Virginia 22210 (703) 525-6873

Copyright 1995 by Joan Mooney
Illustrations copyright 1995 by
The Washington Book Trading Company
All rights reserved.
ISBN 0915168 25-1 $10.95

This book is dedicated
to the people who came with me
Sue, Liz and Chris, Mary Anne, Joe, and Dave,
and to my mother,
who was (as usual) present through it all.

COUNTRY ADVENTURES

Introduction	1
VIRGINIA	3
Hunt Country Stable Tour	5
Manassas and Warrenton	9
Fredericksburg	13
Leesburg	17
Middletown and Belle Grove	20
Waterford Black History Walking Tour	24
Northern Virginia Wineries	28
Shenandoah National Park	31
Skyline Caverns	34
Luray Caverns and New Market	37
Rappahannock River Cruise	41
Charlottesville	45
James River Plantations	50
Williamsburg Black History	56
Chincoteague Pony Penning	61
Tangier Island	64
MARYLAND	69
Ladew Topiary Gardens	71
Ellicott City	74
Havre de Grace	78
New Market	82
Frederick County	85
Carroll County	88
Garrett County	92
The Trail of John Wilkes Booth	96
Annapolis Walking Tour	102
Chestertown and the Eastern Neck	107
Easton Waterfowl Festival	111
Oxford, Cambridge, and St Michael's	115
Snow Hill and Berlin	119
Land of the Crabber, Oysterman, and Farmer	125
WEST VIRGINIA	131
Harpers Ferry	133
Shepherdstown	138
Charles Town	141
Berkeley Springs	144
The Greenbrier	147
Wilderness Railroad	151
Index	154

INTRODUCTION

"Country roads are what I love.

Country roads, innocent of stop signs, advertising billboards, 18-wheel trucks, and the attentions of road graders. We should be collecting them like diamonds because they're not making any more of them. They're a last inheritance from the people who came before us and they lead to places that soothe the souls of city folks. They're our compensation for rush hour traffic."

That's how my mother started the introduction to the first edition of *Country Adventures* 10 years ago, and I can think of no better beginning for the second edition. The things she mentioned, at least, have not changed—the need for urbanites to be soothed is stronger than ever.

The vestiges of the city have sprawled much farther out in the past 10 years. People commute to Washington from Leesburg, Frederick, even Winchester and Fredericksburg. That was one reason this book was revised—to make sure it wasn't leading vacationers to formerly charming small towns that have become part of the suburban sprawl. But people like to live in such spots precisely because of their small town appeal or their historic associations, and so these communities (if they are smart) try to retain their charm. Leesburg is a good example: While it is practically a suburb of Washington now, much about the historic district remains unchanged, and that's what makes it appealing.

One of the things I love about Washington is that it's so easy to get to the countryside: the Shenandoah Mountains, the Chesapeake Bay, the ocean beach at Assateague, the farmland of Carroll County, wineries in the foothills of the mountains, and Civil War battlefields. Within an hour of the city, you can drive on an unpaved road, surrounded by farmland, unable to imagine that the city is so close. Not much farther, if you're lucky, you can catch a glimpse of a bobcat on Skyline Drive. And you can hear a pretty thick country accent just an hour and a half from Washington, in Virginia's northern neck.

Many of these trips can be done in a day. It's nice to know you can be in the country in an hour. But it's even better to take a weekend, stay in one of the myriad bed and breakfasts, and have a mini-vacation that only requires you to drive an hour or two when you're ready to go home.

Everything in the first edition has been checked. I tried to keep the flavor of my mother's writing—after all, she introduced me to many of these places when I accompanied her on research trips for the first book. But, inevitably, some museums have expanded, others have shut down, and a few places can't really be recommended anymore. I have added several new chapters: on black history in Williamsburg, a black history walking tour of Waterford, the plantations along the James River, Virginia wineries, and Garrett County, among others. A few chapters are largely unchanged from the first edition, because little has changed and I didn't think I could improve upon my mother's descriptions. Others are a joint effort between daughter and mother—an interesting exercise when one is alive and the other dead.

The book reflects my personality. If you're the sort of person who likes going to noisy bars in Ocean City in the middle of August, these trips probably aren't your style. I love living in the city, and I love escaping it to places as unlike urban life as possible. In some of the places described here, there is not much to do except watch the boats go by on the river or relax with a good meal before retiring to a four-poster bed. Others have very good museums or historic homes highlighting the lives of unusual individuals like Barbara Fritchie or Harvey Ladew.

If you go on such a weekend, you will be amazed at how easy it is to settle into a slower rhythm, where seeing a bald eagle or staying in a house from 1710 seems more important than whatever was preoccupying you back in the city. If this book has led you to such a place, and frame of mind, then it will have accomplished its purpose.

Joan Mooney

VIRGINIA

Residents of the Washington area who are familiar with the interstate rivalry here may not be surprised at this confession: Growing up in Maryland, I rarely crossed the river to Virginia until I was out of high school. Now I go there nearly every day, although I've been known to mutter crossly that I get lost every time I do.

But here's the news (not news, of course, to residents of the Old Dominion): It's worth it. You only have to drive half an hour or so from downtown D.C. to be in real Virginia countryside, farmland with horses and cows just off the road—and not much farther to be in the mountains. It's a huge state, but there are many lovely trips that can be made in a day or a leisurely weekend from Washington. One of my favorite short trips is to the Virginia wineries just off Interstate 66. Even if you don't drink, the countryside is beautiful and the views, spectacular. Go a little farther, and you're in the Shenandoah Mountains, impressive at

any time but with an unsurpassed color show in the fall.

I love the caves of Virginia. For some reason, I had missed Luray and Skyline Caverns until I wrote this book, and I was like a kid in a candy store, oohing and aahing at the bizarre rock formations along with the hokiest tour guide.

Civil War buffs will feel that they're in heaven in Virginia. Within an hour or so from Washington are the battlefields at New Market, Manassas, and Fredericksburg. The plantations along the James River bring you into a way of life from the Civil War and earlier, with a much more southern feel than just two hours north.

And no one interested in American history should miss Williamsburg. (My favorite rejoinder, when Disney's America was first proposed as a living history museum in Haymarket, was from the person who said, "We already have a living history museum. It's called Williamsburg.") Learn how you can see it from the perspective of the black people who made up more than half the population there in colonial times.

One of my favorite spots is Chincoteague and the national seashore on Assateague Island, where I go every fall to watch the migrating waterfowl. Another island, this one inhabited, is fascinating because it would be impossible to find a place more different from Washington within a weekend trip: Tangier. Its story is a fascinating one, tied up with making a living from the water, and it has its own quirky charm for visitors.

And it's in the same state as the hunt country around Middleburg, where the horses in the Mellons' stables (which you can visit once a year on Memorial Day weekend) live better lives than some of the people in downtown Washington.

So, despite the slow start I had coming to this northernmost southern state, I can now admit: I love Virginia. Try some of these trips, and you will, too.

HUNT COUNTRY STABLE TOUR

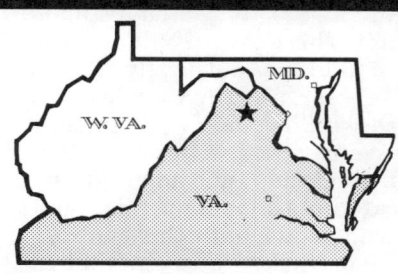

The Virginia hunt country lies just across the river and up from the marble monuments of Washington, but it might as well be light years away. Remember when F. Scott Fitzgerald said "The rich are different from you and me"? For one thing, they *have* their money. Earning a living is something that happens down the pike in Arlington and Alexandria. The business of life here is the horse.

This is the country beloved by the likes of Arthur Godfrey, Jackie Onassis, and, at one time, Elizabeth Taylor: gently rolling pastures defined by stretch-and-riser fences, hawks circling lazily overhead, and the Blue Ridge Mountains blue on the horizon. Wealth speaks quietly here. What you notice is the absence of things, like development, advertising, fast food places, road improvements. Two-lane roads are preferred, and bumpy gravel roads are even better. There's no hurry, and old pickups and sedans are the rule. Nobody here is car proud.

People don't buy houses in towns in the Virginia hunt country. They buy in the heart of the Middleburg Hunt or the Piedmont Hunt or the Old Dominion Hounds. The houses don't change hands much anyway and are hard to see, tucked away behind rail fences and meadows that slope away toward the rolling Blue Ridge. A little red gatekeeper's house at the edge of the property is the only sign that a mile or two up the road lives a Mellon or the niece of General George Patton.

The countryside is reason enough to drive out for a look and a picnic, but the best time to get a glimpse of life among the horsey set is Memorial Day weekend, when in the name of sweet charity, some of the most august homeowners open their stables to the public for a special tour. Even if you've grown out of your horse phase, the trip is an eye-opener.

Upperville, which dates from 1797 and has been designated an Historic Landmark by the Virginia Landmark Commission, is the starting point. Head the car out Route 50 and keep going past rural countryside studded with horses and Black Angus cattle, past Middleburg (which Kennedy made famous when he bought a country house nearby), past the 18th century houses dreaming in the sun with their memories of General J.E.B. Stuart and Mosby's raiders. Keep going 9 miles beyond Middleburg to Upperville and what some have said is the most beautiful church in America, Trinity Episcopal, where you can buy tour tickets.

The church is the gift of Mr. and Mrs. Paul Mellon (women all seem to go by their husbands' names here), who live down the pike, and no expense has been spared to make it lovely. It lifts its spire on the site of an 1842 predecessor, and the view from its cloister is breathtaking. Inside are windows made in Amsterdam, exquisite carving, and 16th century brass from Austria. The bells in the tower were cast in England, and the great bell is inscribed, "These bells are dedicated to the men of this countryside, who, by the skill of their hands, have built this church." You can buy a catered lunch of fried chicken and three-bean salad and picnic at a table out back set with fresh flowers, looking out on the Blue Ridge.

Although the stables that open their doors may differ a little each year, the Middleburg Training Center, where many east coast horses are readied for flat racing, is always on the list. But, it is open only on Saturday. It probably should be your first choice after studying the map on your ticket, because the horses start pounding the turf by 7:30 A.M. and rest up after 10 A.M. Afterward, you can join area horsemen for breakfast in the track kitchen.

Bring a sweater and lean over the rail with the trainers and people clocking the horses' speed. There's no telling who will be standing next to you checking on the new hopefuls, for the track is a blend of muddy boots and horsey chic. Legend has it that a Middleburg matron once arrived to find that her horse's stall needed attention and, wearing a full-length mink over blue jeans, cleaned out the place herself.

From there you might go to Oakley, the estate of Mrs. A. C. Randolph, and usually open for the tour. You can see brood mares like Abbie, who sported a neatly braided mane and thrust out her head to be stroked. You'll soon learn the rather graphic terminology for describing lineage, because ancestry is all in this business: "By Roo Art (the father) out of Lucky Prospector (the mother)." To be considered a thoroughbred, a horse must be bred by natural means—no artificial insemination—and there must be a witness to the horse mounting the mare. If this seems as sadly public as the mating ritual of the pandas at the National Zoo, remember that the horses are very well cared for once they are born.

Part of the Civil War Battle of Upperville was fought in Oakley's front yard. Happily for the legions of Civil War scholars in Virginia, Ida Dulany, who was living in the manor house at the time, left us her diary, describing horses dragging corpses across the grounds. Mrs. Dulany herself carried two wounded men to the house, where they died.

The enormous 1820s home is now occupied by an elderly Mrs. Randolph and her attendants. While she was driven to lunch when we were there, her wheelchair in the back seat, one of the household staff came to the balcony to survey the grounds. Mrs. Randolph is a niece of General George Patton and was quite a horsewoman in her day.

After viewing the brood mares, you can walk up the hill and see some foals. On our trip, we saw Fast Coquette and Say No More, who had been born 3 months earlier. On the way, you pass a nice pond with ducks and swans swimming in it and barn swallows flying overhead. On the way out, a red Porsche passed us with its radio blaring—but, this being Upperville, the music was opera.

If I were a horse, the stables I would undoubtedly choose to live in would be at Rokeby, the Mellons' estate. Always open for the tour, Rokeby is in a league of its own: The parking lot attendants wear jackets and ties, the horses are a bit standoffish, and the stables don't even smell. The stables are immaculate and freshly painted, the hay is thicker, and the horses' coats are smoother. There aren't even any flies.

The volunteers for the tour who sit outside the stables at Rokeby to answer questions are themselves a special breed. One man I talked to, a Washington lawyer with a great interest in horses and Rokeby, said proudly of the horses, "Every one is a potential champion," so they must be treated well. Other volunteers, elderly ladies with big straw hats that made them look like Miss Marple, had stables of their own nearby.

The stalls look out onto a quiet courtyard where a bronze statue of Mill Reef, 1971 European Horse of the Year, contemplates the horizon under an enormous spreading tree. The lineage of the mares' pedigree is framed and posted beside each door, and the gleaming brass fittings are shined every week. Underfoot (or underhoof) is an artificial turf, half rubber and half artificial sod. Arts and Letters and Quadrangle, both winners of the Belmont, were born here. When we went, Sea Hero had just won the Kentucky Derby, and the guest book was filled with congratulatory comments.

On the way out, you will see people hired just to sit in trucks and make sure you don't drive down a private road. They wave cheerily, and as you leave, other minions say, "Thank you for coming," as if they had truly enjoyed your visit and hadn't said that to scores of other strangers all weekend.

Kent Farm, the pied à terre of Jack Kent Cooke, is usually

on the tour, too. The stables line a lovely courtyard, and an unusual indoor trotting track is housed in a tent-shaped building that looks as if it might host a circus. But after Rokeby, it definitely seems nouveau, with touches like director's chairs with "KF" on the back. It's a laid back place for this neighborhood, quiet and pleasant. When you leave by way of a one-lane gravel road with the trees thick on either side, you really feel as if you're in the country.

Middleburg, unofficial capital of this hunt country, is a shopper's paradise, with store windows packed with things for horses and those who ride them. Antiques are big here, 18th century and Victorian, and if you come other than Memorial Day weekend you could make a day of it shopping. The Intimate Fox boutique has hats, shoes, and scarves, and the Papery offers unusual stationery and wooden picture frames. The Antiquarian Book and Autograph Center, just off the main drag at 2 North Madison Street, is small and stuffy, as used bookstores should be, and has some signed first editions from the 19th century, along with such oddments as train tickets used by Charles Dickens, and of course—this being the South—Confederate money.

Then of course there's the Red Fox Inn, claimed to be the second oldest original inn in the country. Here, as everywhere, the fox is king and he snarls from the wall and poses on the huge fireplace mantel, stuffed and looking as if he had defended himself to the last. George Washington sometimes came here when employed as a surveyor, since Chinn's Ordinary, as it was then called, was presided over by his cousin, Joseph Chinn.

The Red Fox tries to keep up the 18th century atmosphere, but if you prefer something more modern (and more affordable), head for Mosby's Tavern, a block away and under the same management. Mosby's has billiards, dancing on weekends, and a menu ranging from sandwiches and salads to Tex Mex. Both can be reached at (703) 687-6301, or, toll-free from the Washington metro area, (703) 478-1808.

For information about the Hunt Country Stable Tour, call (703) 592-3711.

MANASSAS AND WARRENTON

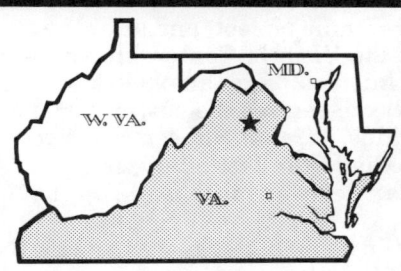

At first what strikes your eye are the split-rail fences and the open sweep of the Virginia countryside. But after a while, you begin to people it in your mind with young men firing up the cannons, horses rearing up in fright, and General Jackson standing there like a stone wall. And, though you're looking at Manassas more than 130 years after the battles, the Civil War no longer seems so long ago. It isn't, to people in these parts.

The cannons are silent now at Manassas National Battlefield Park in northern Virginia, but the Park Service does a splendid job of evoking what happened here in 1861 and 1862. Start with the interpretive slide program that the Visitors Center runs in its small theater and you'll get a good perspective on those long-ago summer battles. The southern-accented voice-over reading from a letter by J.W. Reid in the South Carolina regiment describes the horrors of battle in no uncertain terms.

If you thought the Civil War was fought between the Blue and Gray, you're in for a shock when you see the array of uniforms chosen from the 200 different ones worn in that first battle. It was clearly a task to tell friend from enemy. But it's the Ohio surgeon's battle case, with its small saw for amputations, that brings home this war, in which 400,000 men were lost—more than in any other U.S. war. Learn about Captain James Ricketts, who fell beside his guns in the field; his wife came out to nurse him, and the bowl she brought for him to eat from is on display. You can also see a fan belonging to Judith Carter Henry, the 85-year-old civilian casualty of the First Battle of Manassas.

Mrs. Henry was an invalid who was born a mile from the battlefield and, for 35 years of her long life, lived in the white farmhouse you can see from the Visitors Center. Told to evacuate, she refused and was eventually killed by a stray mortar shell. Her house survived and they buried her in the side yard overlooking the valley. You can see it on the self-guided tour.

Downstairs at the Visitors Center, you see the other side of battlefield life: a piece of hard tack, a bread ration that the label says is "probably not much harder today than it was when it was made in 1861." Also on display is a twist of chewing tobacco and

10   a clay pipe—the soldiers' recreation on the field of battle.

There's a small fee to tour the battlefield (like every other place, the Park Service is in a budget crunch), and in return you get an informative map. The tour is a mile on foot, and after that you can see the rest by car. Near the Visitors Center, stop and have a look at the monument to Union soldiers, an obelisk surrounded by large bullets. Behind it, you can see the post-and-rail fences and the Blue Ridge Mountains. It is an odd sensation to stand in the peaceful expanse of a Civil War battlefield, so quiet today, trying to imagine the furor and carnage that made up the scene on the day of battle.

If the weather's fine, there could be no better place to picnic than the official picnic area just off the little country road across from Matthews Hill, where Confederate Colonel Nathan Evans tried to stop the Union advance.

Part of the driving tour is the Stone House, used as a field hospital in both battles, usually open daily from Memorial Day to Labor Day and weekends in the spring and fall. It's worth putting this old house on your itinerary, but check ahead to make sure it's open; call (703) 754-1861 (you can remember the number because it's the year of the first battle). A look inside the house is worth six books on the history of the battle.

The old house started life in the 1820s as an inn selling hard liquor to hard men who drove wagons along the turnpike. In 1862 Union soldiers took it over as a hospital; you can see a reconstructed operating room, the operating table a litter on barrels, covered with bloodstained blankets. Through the hand-blown window glass, the surgeons must have been able to see the fighting as they hacked away at their chloroformed, strapped-down patients, well over half of whom had arm and leg wounds for which amputation was the only known answer. When they were at last released from the table, survival was chancy. Medicine of the time knew little or nothing about how to control "surgical fever."

If you're curious to learn more about the town of Manassas, not just the battle that made it famous, stop at the Manassas Museum. The exhibits include a fair amount of black history; the Northern Virginia Piedmont had a large population of free blacks in the 1800s. You can follow the lives of typical area residents. Ann Bailey Marsteller, born in 1798 and a slave owner, is juxtaposed next to Sarah, a composite slave. Ms. Marsteller's life is illustrated with a sampler and a dressing glass, while Sarah is represented by leg irons and a soap kettle.

The video "A Community at War" is only 8 minutes long and is worth a look. It tells the history of the town and the battle and is notable for showing the desecration of war instead of glorifying it (very different from the treatment of the Battle of New Market you will find in the video at the New Market museum). In 1861, in the first battle of Manassas, 4,700 men were killed or injured; in the second battle a year later, 20,000 men were killed. Nearly every house, barn, fence, and tree was destroyed, and afterward the town had to rebuild from scratch. Although it wasn't that far from the nation's capital, Manassas was a rural outpost with ordinances decreeing that cattle and sheep must be off the streets after 9 o'clock at night.

James Robinson, a free black, became the owner of much of the land in the battlefield. One of his sons survived the war and came home as a free man in 1888. It was not until the 1940s that his descendants sold the land to the U.S. government and the park was created.

If you have a little more time, drive 17 miles down Route 29 (the Warrenton Turnpike) to Warrenton, known today as one of the homes of Virginia's horsey set, but a town that goes back to 1759 and well remembers Manassas and the Civil War.

On Warren Green here, General McClellan said farewell to his troops after being relieved of his command, and in the Confederate cemetery down the hill sleeps Colonel John Mosby, the partisan leader whose exploits are legend. Warrenton sent every able-bodied man she could muster into the Confederate Army and drew Union fire throughout the war.

A self-guided walking tour, available from the Fauquier Historical Society, (703) 347-5525, will lead you through the narrow, hilly streets and brick sidewalks of the historic section. The Court House is especially beautiful, an 1893 replica of the original 1791 building. Behind it is the Old Jail Museum, where Fauquier County keeps its historic souvenirs, one of the few preserved jails in the state. Close by is the old Warren Green Hotel, where Lafayette was entertained in 1825 and Wallis Simpson stayed while awaiting her divorce so she could marry the Duke of Windsor. It now houses county offices.

On Waterloo Street, the houses are grand old dowagers from another century. Number 67 has been turned into an attractive restaurant, Napoleon's. It once belonged to Civil War General Hunton and is one of the 1830s homes that survived Warrenton's disastrous fire of 1909. You can have lunch or dinner in the light, airy back room, on the patio just outside, or go for a classier dinner in the room up front (appropriate attire requested). The menu offers everything from soups and sandwiches to fish and steak.

In this part of the world the 1900s are only yesterday, but

in nearby Bealeton the planes performing in the Flying Circus Air Show are antiques by any other standard. Planes from aviation's barnstorming days take to the air every Sunday at 2 P.M. from May through October to perform death-defying barrel rolls and dives for spectators brought up in the age of jets. Vintage-plane buffs meet here weekly to tie on a white silk aviator's scarf and goggles and live the old days again in the open planes. Dogfights, wing-walking, and parachute jumps will stimulate your pulse rate better than jogging.

    A bonus in this trip back into history is the pretty Warrenton Turnpike, once crowded with the carriages of spectators out from Washington to see the rebellion put down. At least for part of the way from Manassas, it pushes through the kind of countryside you don't see much anymore, innocent of advertising, an unspoiled treasure of the Old Dominion.

FREDERICKSBURG

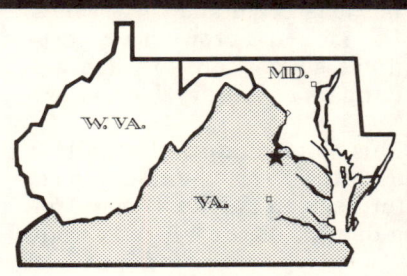

That Fredericksburg is home to many Washington commuters says a lot about the town's charm. It is just as pleasant to visit. The residents are proud to share their town's history, and their enthusiasm is contagious. A short walk down Caroline Street tells you immediately that the Civil War was the big event here. But the historic buildings date back to the 1700s, and George Washington was part of the early history (Fredericksburg's motto is, "George Washington slept a lot of places, but he lived here").

To orient yourself, stop at the Visitors Center on Caroline Street, well-marked from the entrance into town. Not only is it the most helpful visitors center I have ever been in, but you can also get a "Visitor" sign for your car that enables you to park free on the street all day (imagine *that* in Washington). Our helpful assistant at the center said proudly of her hometown, "All the buildings are restored, not rebuilt—and that's more than Williamsburg can say." You can get a map with a walking or driving tour; everything in the historic district is an easy walk. If you plan to visit several places, you will get a discount if you buy a block ticket for admission to seven different historic sites.

Fredericksburg's most famous home is Kenmore, built by Fielding Lewis for himself and his wife Betty, George Washington's sister. His first wife was Catherine, Betty's cousin, but when she died, he married Betty a few months later; both women were second cousins to Lewis. Intermarriage was apparently not as much of a taboo then.

You enter Kenmore through a separate gallery, with forbidding looking family portraits, including one of Betty Washington Lewis, who looked so much like her brother George that it was a joke to clothe her in military cloak and hat and imagine the troops saluting her. You can study the family tree of the Fielding Lewises, a pen and ink drawing with leaves drawn in and more than 100 names, up to Queen Elizabeth II.

From the outside, the large brick house doesn't look like anything fancy, although it is impressively surrounded by dogwood and oak and winding paths connecting the buildings. But inside, its dining room has been declared one of the hundred most beautiful rooms in America. Its finest feature is the molded plaster ceiling, painstakingly done by hand by an unidentified "stucco man" whom the Lewises shared with the Washingtons at Mount Vernon. Over the mantel is a bas relief showing scenes from Aesop's Fables; the legend of the fox and crow was reportedly included at George Washington's suggestion, to warn his young nieces and nephews of the dangers of flattery. They were a stern lot, our forefathers.

Washington often dined with his sister and brother-in-law at Kenmore, including the night in March 1775 when he was on his way home to Mount Vernon after hearing Patrick Henry proclaim, "Give me liberty or give me death!" at the Virginia Convention in Richmond.

But Lewis was a better patriot than he was a money manager. He kept advancing his personal funds to pay for the expenses of the Fredericksburg Gunnery and his shipping business. Although he still had thousands of acres, a boat, and warehouses when he died, he was monetarily poor. Betty, left with her three youngest children, managed to run the plantation for 14 more years.

Several visitors claim to have seen Fielding Lewis's ghost at Kenmore, wearing a worried expression and dressed in Revolutionary era clothes. Sometimes he appears brooding over a pile of papers, thought perhaps to be creditors' bills.

The only way you can see Kenmore is with a tour guide, and ours was rather stern and schoolmarmish, as if she knew that Kenmore is the main attraction in town, now as it was 200 years earlier. Don't worry—you can revive yourself afterward with a visit to the kitchen (a separate building because of the danger of the open fire), where you will be served tea and gingerbread from the same recipe Mary Washington (George and Betty's mother) used when she served General Lafayette.

Kenmore was almost not left standing for us to see. The property changed hands ten times after Betty Lewis's death, and in 1919 was bought by a contractor who planned to cut up the property into little houses. The ladies of Fredericksburg banded together to save Kenmore, and the owner gave them a seemingly impossible 6 months to come up with a $10,000 down payment. They held bake sales and church bazaars and even sold Mary Washington's gingerbread recipe. The lease was signed 6 years later, and the Kenmore Association still runs the estate.

You could spend a few days tracing colonial and Civil War history in Fredericksburg, but one museum, the Rising Sun Tavern, is a must. The tour guides play the part of tavern wenches, indentured servants who were too poor to pay their passage from England and so agreed to work a certain number of years in exchange for being brought to the colonies. Taking us back to the years the tavern was open, from 1792 to 1827, our guide told us her job was a good one because she only works 18 hours a day, 7 days a week. Plus, she gets two nice outfits a year and a pair of shoes every 4 years.

The women dined and slept separately from the men, and our tavern wench said approvingly, "I see all you ladies brought your needlework. We assured the gentlemen we would keep you busy and productive." The women were on a tight schedule: dinner at 4:30 P.M. and upstairs to the common bedroom at 6:30 P.M., to be awakened around 12:30 A.M. to prepare for the stagecoach, which left for the next tavern at 2 A.M. The extra time was needed to help the women squeeze into their corsets.

A hip bath was available for the tavern's guests, but people only took baths in July and August because of the fear of consumption. Things must have gotten pretty ripe the rest of the year—think of June in Virginia—because the men slept five to a bed. But not to worry—the rule that they had to keep their boots on in bed was strictly enforced, since they slept head to toe.

Next, walk down to Hugh Mercer's apothecary to learn how people coped before the advent of penicillin and anesthesia. We started with the herbs in the front room, hearing that lavender tea cures sleeplessness, and that we should chew flax seeds for diarrhea and snake root for pleurisy. Dr. Mercer recommended that his patients smoke so they could cough and get rid of their phlegm. Ginseng was reputed to have an even more important power: to "cheer a man with a bad wife," as one plantation owner wrote.

Dr. Mercer was famous for his bleeding, and a bleeding chart is posted on the wall of the back room. He took one quart of blood, being careful to cut lengthwise because crosswise cuts tend to bleed on and on. The usual bleeding tool was leeches, and some modern hospitals have shown a renewed interest in how leeches were used—"not in me if I know it," said our friend at the visitors center with some feeling.

Dr. Mercer didn't like to do surgery because the patient usually died, and then the family would complain to the church. He did do amputations, but they had to be finished in four minutes or the patient would go into shock. A box of sawdust lay on the floor to catch the amputated limb. Somehow, it makes our current health care crisis seem a little less terrible.

Even if you're not a Civil War buff, you ought to visit the Fredericksburg battlefields and national cemetery. Fifteen thousand Union soldiers are buried there, more than 80 percent of them unknown. Four major Civil War battles were fought here on the road between Washington and Richmond, and the town changed hands seven times. More than 100,000 men lost their lives. It brings home the losses of war on a human scale as you wander among the old grave markers, past the monument at the entrance dedicated to the Fifth Corps.

The Civil War doesn't seem to be quite finished in Fredericksburg. Civil War bullets are fairly common in the antique and junk shops, but one store has a sign advertising "Artifacts of America's Second War of Independence."

When you're ready to ease back into the 20th century, the shops along Caroline Street are good for browsing. The Made in Virginia Store has everything from Virginia hams to wooden pull toys to Civil War prints, and the Collector's Den displays a jumbled assortment of arrowheads, baseball cards, and a large shark's jaw.

There are several antique stores—some bargains, some overpriced, and some junk—and myriad used and rare book shops. We knew we weren't in Washington anymore when we saw a coin box on top of the book carts outside one store so you could leave money for what you bought.

Fredericksburg has a good variety of restaurants. The Kenmore Inn (where you can stay, if you want to make a weekend of it), at 1200 Princess Anne Street, was built by Fielding Lewis's father and survived the battle of Fredericksburg intact, although it was heavily shelled. It now serves lunch and dinner in a pleasant dining room with two big fireplaces.

Other good, fancy restaurants are La Petit Auberge, 311 William Street, and Le LaFayette, 623 Caroline Street. For more casual fare, try Allman's Bar BQ, 2000 Augustine Avenue, outside the historic district, or, on Caroline Street, Spanky's or Spirits. Spanky's is a cafe/deli with sandwiches named after sports heroes, and Spirits serves sandwiches and pizza in a cozy room with fireplaces and exposed brick walls.

Smythe's Cottage, 303 Fauquier Street, serves southern food (and the best apple turnovers I've ever had) in an old blacksmith's home and stable. The food was good, but the service was extremely slow.

Wondering why a portrait of Ulysses S. Grant was hung upside down in the bar, we encountered more lingering Civil War feelings. The restaurant's original owner's great-great grandfather was a scout for J.E.B. Stuart and refused to dig entrenchments for the Union Army when he was a prisoner. As punishment, he was hung by his thumbs.

Now, poor Grant is gazing at the bourbon upside down, like Tantalus. Even after all these years, revenge is sweet.

LEESBURG

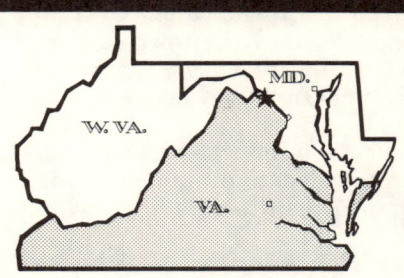

The statement in this book's first edition, "Route 7 off the Washington Beltway does not have charm," seems like a laughable understatement 10 years later. But it's still worth following Route 7 to drive to Leesburg. (For a more pleasant alternative, take Route 50 to Route 15.) Even though a good portion of Leesburg's population now commutes to Washington or closer suburbs, it has kept its feeling of a small rural town where neighborhoods are named after incidents from horse-and-buggy days. While Leesburg has plenty of history, it isn't overflowing with museums and Civil War shops the way, say, Fredericksburg is (some would consider this an advantage). It gets my award for being the closest place to Washington (less than an hour from downtown) that is slow-paced enough to feel like a trip out of city.

Start at the Visitors Center in Market Station, a multi-roofed, wooden mini-mall off Loudoun Street, with several shops and restaurants on the site of an old mill. This neighborhood is called Vinegar Hill, after a former slave who drove through town in a horse-drawn wagon in the 1860s with a load of apple cider that spilled and turned to vinegar in the summer sun, leaving a smell that lingered for months.

The people at the visitors center can give you a map and point you up the street a couple of blocks to the historic district, where the Loudoun Museum sells a booklet outlining a walking tour around the town's old homes and its imposing courthouse. The courthouse was first built in 1759 and has been replaced twice since then, most recently in 1894. Court Days were held there on the second Monday of March, June, August, and November or December. Now, August Court Days, usually the third weekend in August, commemorate the practice with a craft fair, period marching bands, and a re-enactment of the 18th century judicial court.

Old houses in Leesburg lean against each other, and large trees push up the bricks in the sidewalk. Park your car and walk around the old homes and shops. The past is everywhere: You'll find a stucco building from 1790 that now houses offices, and local realtors are housed in an old fieldstone building.

Leesburg was laid out 17 years before the Declaration of

Independence was signed. Prisoners were allowed to walk free if they did not go outside a 10-acre area between Cornwall and Royal Streets. In its early years, the town was called Georgetown after King George of England. Perhaps the town fathers could see which way the tide was turning, because a few years later, the town was renamed for Francis Lightfoot Lee, a signer of the Declaration.

Lafayette dined at the Laurel Brigade Inn when he was visiting James Monroe. You can eat in the elegant dining room and stay in one of the antique-furnished rooms upstairs, then wander through the gardens out back.

Or you could stay at the Norris House Inn, an 1806 house that originally belonged to the Norris family, Leesburg's most prominent early builders. It has been restored by Pat McMurray, a native Californian who traced her roots back to Loudoun County, bought the Norris house, and changed the decor from Victorian to Federal to match her lighter California sensibilities. Mrs. McMurray and her husband also own the Limelight, an excellent restaurant across the street. Sometimes they serve afternoon tea in the Stone House Tea Room next door, the building that was George Washington's headquarters during the French-Indian War.

When you're ready to get back in your car, you only need to go a mile to Morven Park, the home of Maryland Governor Thomas Swann in the 19th century and Virginia Governor Westmoreland Davis in the early 20th. These men clearly liked things nice. The 1,200-acre farm, famous for its boxwood gardens, is the site of a 28-room mansion whose front entrance boasts Greek columns 3 feet thick, flanked by fierce black lions. Half the rooms were being renovated while we were there and should be in sparkling condition by now. You'll find everything from 16th century Flemish tapestries to art nouveau.

Everything is on a grand scale, even the magnolia trees by the parking lot. The place gives the feeling of a *Gone With the Wind* crumbling aristocracy. Pause on one of the benches scattered around the property to look out over the gentle rolling hills and inhale the smell of boxwood. Bring a picnic if you like (Virginia Vintners in the historic district sells sandwiches, cheese, and delicious homemade bread).

Six miles from Leesburg on Route 15 is another historic home, Oatlands. It is an anomaly, an 1800s house with 1900s furnishings. It was built by George Carter about 1800 on what was originally 5,000 acres, a present from his father on his 21st birthday. He lived there for most of his life in solitary splendor. Not until he was 60, and a widow who had had a carriage accident came knocking at the door, did he succumb to marriage.

Nine years later he was dead. After his wife returned to her girlhood home, Oatlands became a billet for Confederate troops. At the close of the war, one of Carter's sons came here with his wife to live, bringing with him his widowed mother. But money was such a problem that eventually all furniture except the massive sideboard in the dining room was sold. The current beautiful furnishings are those brought to the house by William Corcoran Eustis, grandson of the founder of the Corcoran Gallery and Riggs National Bank, who journeyed out from Washington with his wife one day in 1903 and bought the property without even seeing the inside. After their deaths, Oatlands was given by their daughters to the National Trust.

Eustis was a man whose life revolved around horses; Oatlands, deep in the heart of horse country, reflects his love. It periodically opens its doors to host horsey events. Eustis's hunting pinks are forever laid out ready on the bed, and hoofs from his favorite mounts have been fashioned into an inkwell and a stamp box.

Elegance is the hallmark in this house, which is always full of flowers. The knife boxes on the Carter sideboard hold silver service for 20, and the dessert plates on the dining room table were bought from the heirs of George Washington. Among the portraits and drawings that hang by wires from the moldings in the turn-of-the-century manner are four Piranese engravings. The octagon sitting room, a favorite of Edith Eustis, is a jewel.

The intricate and beautiful plaster moldings of Oatlands are still intact. The Corinthian capitals of the front columns are at eye level from an upstairs window, where a close look shows sparrows nesting happily in their leaves. The columns came by ship from New York to Alexandria and from there by ox cart.

The formal gardens, inspired by the Italian models but typically Virginian, were restored by Edith Eustis and are said to be among Virginia's finest. Primarily green gardens, they feature English boxwood as well as a large rose garden, a reflecting pool, and a tea house built by Mrs. Eustis. Oatlands is open from late March to late December, with special events like point-to-point races and Draft Horse and Mule Day; call (703) 777-3174.

To keep the mood a little longer, go back to Washington by the *General Jubal Early*, a Civil War ferry boat that Lee and J.E.B. Stuart once used to cross the Potomac with their armies. It's known as White's Ferry and still plies the river every 15 minutes from a point 4 miles north of Leesburg off Route 15 on Route 655, from 6 A.M. to 11 P.M. It takes you and your car in slow dignified fashion to the Maryland side.

MIDDLETOWN AND BELLE GROVE

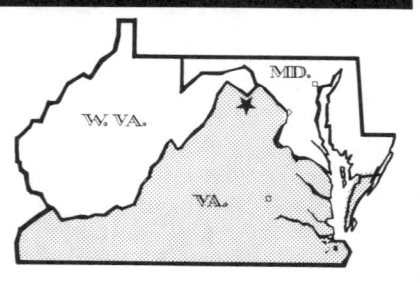

A pleasant drive from Washington out Route 50 will allow you to steep yourself in the turn of the century—the 19th century. You can visit Belle Grove plantation, one of my favorites, with beautiful mountain views on all sides. When you're ready for a large and good meal, stop by the Wayside Inn, as travelers have been doing since 1797. If you decide to stay the night there, you can stop off the next day at Shenandoah Vineyards.

If you go in the fall, here's an added bonus: Driving around this area will give you wonderful views of the changing colors on the Blue Ridge and Massanutten Mountains, minus the crowds on Skyline Drive.

Drive out Route 50 to get there, past Virginia's Hunt Country with its spacious farms, past villages like Aldie and Paris that seem thousands of miles from the city you left behind. You'll probably want to stop at a roadside stand on the way and buy cider and mums if it's fall, or tomatoes and corn if it's summer.

In a little over an hour, you will be in Middletown on Route 11. A mile past the center of town is Belle Grove. While it may not be as grand as some of the more famous plantations along the James River, Belle Grove is appealing because it is less commercial. Our volunteer guide was an affable woman who was clearly fascinated by her subject, not just a hired hand reciting her lines by rote.

Construction of Belle Grove began in 1794 for Major Isaac Hite, Jr., who was married to Nelly Conway Madison, the sister of the future president. The connection paid off when Madison asked his friend Thomas Jefferson for advice in designing Belle Grove. Jefferson's influence can be seen in the pavilion style architecture and interior elements such as the skylight over the front door.

The house is made of local limestone from Major Hite's quarries. Each stone was hand-chiseled at great expense to create a uniform surface. The Colonial homebuilders didn't know that cinder blocks would be invented and make us in the 20th century think that the rough-hewn stones in the back look much nicer than the hand-chiseled ones.

But inside, the house has many 18th century touches that

impress us modern folk. The ceilings are extremely high —impractical as this was in the winter, when all the heat from the fireplaces rose to the top of the rooms—because Mr. Jefferson thought this a suitable status symbol to borrow from Europe.

There are beautiful woodwork patterns around the perimeter of most of the rooms, painstakingly carved by hand over who knows how many hours. But people of that time were accustomed to intensive labor. Each piece of the Hites's linen was numbered and dated, so they would know when it would have to be replaced. They needed plenty of advance notice because they had to grow the flax, spin it, and dye it—an enormous amount of work was required to create a new sheet.

The upkeep is even more impressive when you consider that the Hites had 12 children, all of whom grew to adulthood. For a long time this family of 14 got by with two bedrooms, until they added another wing in the mid-19th century.

Wonderful bits of the past are on display. Sarah Hite's wedding dress is in a glass case, and although it was full length, it looks like a child's size—apparently people really were much shorter then. Major Hite's commission to the Army, signed by Patrick Henry, is in another case, along with a china cup and bits of crockery found in the field outside the house. Our guide thinks that before the days of trash collection, people just threw their discarded objects outside. "We find all sorts of things in our field," she says.

Of course no old home in these parts would be complete without its Civil War connection. You will find here a handsome grandfather clock that belonged to General Jubal Early, head of the Confederate forces during the Battle of Cedar Creek. This battle, a pivotal one (weren't they all?), took place nearby on October 19, 1864, and is re-enacted every October. Belle Grove was the headquarters of Union General Philip Sheridan. Apparent victory in the battle went back and forth between the two sides, but in the end the Confederate forces, far outnumbered, were defeated.

Besides his quarries, Major Hite owned some mills and a general store, and at one point he had 103 slaves to keep everything going. Many of them worked on the farm, which in the first part of the 19th century had 7,500 acres. Quite a few slaves must have been kept busy in the winter kitchen, which is preserved downstairs. As you can see by the fact that the cook's bed is in the kitchen, this was a 24-hour-a-day job. The kitchen fire was kept going all the time because the other fires in the house were started from that one. Fresh bread was baked for every meal in the beehive ovens, and often beaten biscuits, too. After you had beaten them vigorously with a stick, "Your arm knew what you had been doing," our guide said.

Cooking over the hearth was pretty low-tech. To cook a chicken, you would tie it to a string, twist it around several times, and let it roast evenly as it unwound. Refrigeration depended on the weather. If the creek didn't freeze, there was no ice.

Naturally such a house would have a ghost. Harriet Robinson, the slave and mistress of Benjamin Cooley, who owned Belle Grove in the 1860s, resented his new wife Hettie and was convicted of her murder on purely circumstantial evidence. Because she was pregnant, Ms. Robinson was not executed, but Hettie's ghost is said to walk the premises still. She was once reportedly seen by a workman who said he was confounded to watch her walk straight through a wall and ascend. It seems she was only using the stairs that had been there in her time.

When you have finished your tour of Belle Grove, you may want to sit in back at the picnic tables, put there for school groups but handy for adults, too. That view of the mountains never gets old.

All this history and talk of cooking will have helped you work up an appetite, and you will be ready for a meal at the Wayside Inn. Famous in the area, it's well marked and right on Route 11 in Middletown. The management has done an excellent job of restoring the inn, which was nearly gutted in a 1985 fire.

In the inn's early days, a servant boy would be sent up the hill to watch for a cloud of dust on the horizon, which might signal travelers in need of hot food. Although Route 11 is a little noisier now than when it was known as the Valley Pike and saw only stagecoach traffic, it is still quite pleasant to sit in the rockers on the inn's front porch and watch the world go by. If the weather is inclement, you can retire to the sitting room, furnished with antiques and old books.

The colonial theme continues in the dining room, with dark wood floor and ceiling beams, and waiters and waitresses in 18th century garb. But the inn never veers over into hokiness the way some places do—and there's no chicken roasted on a twisted string. The place would be fun anyway, but as a bonus, the food is quite good. Every table gets a delicious loaf of homemade bread (my choice over beaten biscuits any day), and you will want to try the peanut soup, or if you're lucky, the special when we were there: cheddar-ale soup. Entrees are things like country ham and smothered chicken (baked for a couple of hours in wine and its own juices). Of course, you will want some pecan pie or chocolate cake for dessert, and before you know it, you're sodden with food (but happy).

Although it's an easy drive back home from here, consider staying overnight at the inn. It has 29 rooms, furnished with antiques, many with four-poster beds. Progress was inevitable, and most now have phones and TVs. (The up side is that the inn now takes credit cards.)

To continue the theme of food and drink, drive south on Interstate 81 to Route 675 and Shenandoah Vineyards in Edinburg. When her husband James had a heart attack, owner Emma Randel moved here to the farm where her mother was born, after the Randels decided Virginia would be a good place for him to recover. Although James died several years ago, Emma has continued the winery they started and is active in the Virginia Wineries Association. Besides tastings and self-guided tours, Shenandoah Vineyards has picnic tables and a beautiful view of the Blue Ridge Mountains. There's a pig roast every July, if you like that sort of thing.

Belle Grove is open from mid-March through mid-November from 10 A.M. to 4 P.M. daily and 1 P.M. to 5 P.M. Sunday; call (703) 869-2028. The Wayside Inn's phone is (703) 869-1797, and Shenandoah Vineyards' is (703) 984-8699.

WATERFORD BLACK HISTORY WALKING TOUR

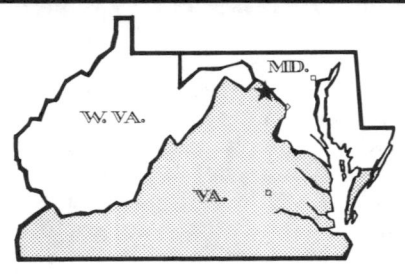

To longtime Waterford resident Bronwen Souders, following the trail of black history in the 260-year-old village of Waterford, Virginia, is like a treasure hunt. She has combed through property deeds in the courthouse, old census rolls, and wills, and has interviewed old and former residents. Now she eagerly shares the fruits of her research on a guided Black History Walking Tour, one of the offerings of the Waterford Foundation.

Waterford is unusual for many reasons, one being that there were always more free blacks than slaves there, partly because of the large number of Quakers, who were abolitionists. But even more important was the abundance of jobs in the then-prosperous commercial center of Waterford and its surrounding farms. While the census listed black men as laborers and women as domestics, they actually had skilled jobs as carpenters, bricklayers, fence builders, merchants, tanners, stonemasons, midwives, seamstresses, and teachers. A 70-year-old black woman who grew up in Waterford told Ms. Souders, "Living in Waterford was not like living anywhere else. We didn't know we were different until we left."

Today, the entire village, a short drive from Leesburg, is a National Historic Landmark, and it's not too different from the way it was 200 years ago. Of the original houses, none is left, though parts of them are. The houses on Main Street are intact, dating from 1800 or later. Only 200 people live in the village now, though the population mushroomed to 400 in the 1800s. You can see cows grazing in a field just off one of the village streets. When you accompany a walking tour leader through the village, she waves to everyone you pass—it's not hard to know your neighbors in a place that small.

Waterford was founded in 1733 by Quakers from Pennsylvania, rather than by Virginia settlers from the east, like neighboring towns, which had a tobacco slave culture. Waterford's history was much influenced by the Quakers. The village was founded because of the mill, and many of the residents worked at the mill or as grain farmers, or both. There's still a mill at the same site on Main Street, though not the original one. This one dates from the 1840s and was used until the 1940s.

Ms. Souders says excitedly that a few months ago, the great-great granddaughter of three of the early millers released the recorded accounts of the mill book from the 1830s to the 1870s, which includes the work record of many of the black people in town. While wealthy whites paid for goods with cash, black families and poor whites paid with their labor, with work at the mill (which earned $100 a year) being exchanged for useful commodities like corn. The mill book has an account page for each person, showing when he took a day to haul grain to Point of Rocks, Maryland, or took time off to go to Court Days in Leesburg. Ms. Souders says of the mill, "It wasn't just a place to work; it was the center of the village."

Across from the mill is the John Wesley Community Church, built in 1890 for the growing congregation of the African Methodist Episcopal Church. (Before that, worshipers had used the school on Second Street for services.) The church members gave ice cream socials and barbecue suppers for years to pay it off—it's a good-sized Gothic revival building.

In the 1800s, many blacks worked in the pits of the tan yard, next to the church. Once the train station was opened in Clarke's Gap in 1870, the Washington markets were more accessible, and there was no longer a need to produce leather locally, so the tan yard was closed. You can still see what's left of the pits.

Because of its Quaker heritage, Waterford was something of an anomaly during the Civil War. In 1861, the village voted 221 to 36 against secession, though Loudoun County favored it 2 to 1. Because of his Unionist sympathies, Samuel Means, the owner of the mill, had it and his livestock and other investments confiscated. In 1861, he was forced to flee to Maryland, and the Confederates offered a $5,000 reward for his capture. The following year, Secretary of War Edwin Stanton asked Means to raise a company from his friends and neighbors, and he recruited the Loudoun Rangers, the only organized Union troop from Virginia.

One black survivor of the Civil War, Richard Edward Cullins, came back to Waterford to be a stonemason and lived for years on Main Street, where today only the ruins of his house are standing. As a 16-year-old drummer boy, Cullins was lucky to survive the Fort Pillow massacre in Tennessee. Scores of men were killed, including many blacks. The incident was so bloody that a congressional investigation followed.

Cullins's house collapsed 20 years ago. Loudoun County students excavated it and set up an exhibit at the Waterford Crafts Fair one year, displaying the slate pencils, shards of pottery, and Civil War uniform buttons they had found.

From Main Street, turn down Second Street, to the part of the village called New Town in 1800, to the Second Street School. The Quakers built this as a public school for blacks in 1868, and for years it was a one-room schoolhouse for kindergarten through eighth grade. Today, the Waterford Foundation does living history programs there, with third and fourth graders taking on the roles of 19th century black Waterford schoolchildren. The children are told to thank their parents for providing their schoolbooks, because the state of Virginia only provided them for white children. On the wall is a wonderful old class photo, found by the nephew of one of the students, of a large group of children accompanied by a stern-looking teacher in a three-piece suit, his hat nearby.

When Ms. Souders was a docent at the Second Street School, she talked to some descendants of the children who had been students there. That's when she got interested in Waterford's black history and applied for grants to find out more.

One connection to the school was Daniel Webster "Web" Minor, a black Waterford resident who bought a house on Main Street at an auction in 1873. He served with the Loudoun Rangers during the Civil War, then returned to the village to marry and work as a builder of post-and-rail fences, and to serve on the first board of directors of the Second Street School.

Ms. Souders's research into the village's black history has meant much poring over old censuses and sometimes, just plain luck. Waterford is the kind of place where, even years after people have moved away, they write back with questions or information. A few years ago, the village got a letter from Mr. Adolphus Dean in Ohio, asking for pictures of Waterford in the 1920s, when he was a boy there. The letter went to the Waterford Foundation, and Ms. Souders took a chance and called him to ask if he was related to George and Elizabeth Dean.

"There was dead silence on the other end," she says. "Then he said, 'How did you know? Those were my grandparents.'" She knew the name from the census.

After you have passed the Second Street School, turn left and go up to High Street. Two churches face each other across the street at the top of the hill: the Presbyterian church, built in the 1880s when the previous one burned, and the Quaker meetinghouse dating from 1761. Today, there are so few members of the Society of Friends left in Waterford that the meetinghouse is no longer used.

Across the street from the churches, a developer recently proposed building a 66-house development—an idea strongly opposed by the Waterford Foundation. In the end, they worked out a compromise: The Foundation raised $200,000 to buy most of the land ($100,000 from the proceeds of the Crafts Fair and $100,000 from the state). Now, only 16 houses will be built on the site.

A little farther on, you can find three cemeteries, for whites, blacks, and Quakers. The black cemetery was so poorly kept until 10 years ago that although Ms. Souders was told it was there, she didn't believe it because she couldn't find it. Now, it has been cleaned up by the Eagle Scouts, and you can see stone markers, though none is earlier than 1854. Web Minor is buried there, as are four other black Civil War veterans.

At the top of the hill on the way to the cemeteries is the old high school that served white children until the early 1930s, when Loudoun County began bussing them to a segregated school in Leesburg. Today, all of Waterford's high school students attend integrated school in Leesburg. While the population was 25 percent black until the 1950s, at last count, only three black people lived in the village.

Research continues on the role of Waterford's black citizens in its past. One year recently the village held a black family reunion, and many of Waterford's former residents came. Ms. Souders (who is white) was also there, and an older black woman asked her, "No offense, ma'am, but why are you doing this?" The quest started as a way to bolster the living history program at the Second Street School, and now it has become a mission.

If you want to take the Waterford Black History Walking Tour, call the Waterford Foundation at (703) 882-3018 to make a reservation; a donation is requested. If you want to explore the village on your own, pick up a general walking tour brochure at the Corner Store in the center of the village, where three roads meet. On weekdays, you can visit the Foundation at the Waterford Tin Shop on the corner of Second and Main Streets.

There are no shops to speak of in Waterford; only three to four spaces are even zoned for commercial use. But you will find a lovely feeling of serenity, and if you want to savor it longer, you can stay at The Pink House, (703) 882-3453, which has three rooms and a magnificent terraced formal garden. Waterford also has a rather famous crafts fair every October; call the Foundation for information.

NORTHERN VIRGINIA WINERIES

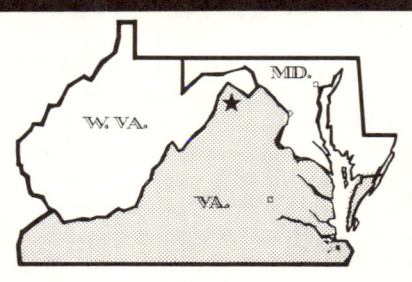

Thomas Jefferson would be pleased and proud to see the explosion of wineries in his native state. He loved good wine and was convinced that Virginia soil was conducive to vineyards, even though his own efforts never bore fruit. The idea lay dormant for a couple hundred years. Farfelu Vineyard in Flint Hill became the first licensed farm winery in the state in 1974; now, Virginia has more than 40, many of them only an hour from Washington. The state even has its own viticulturist and state oenologist.

There must be a certain winery landscaping that is taught in the class for winery architects. It is good for the vines (and the visitors) to be in the hills because the soil drains well, being loamy, unlike the clayey soil found elsewhere in northern Virginia. Those wineries not actually in the mountains are at least in the hills with a view of mountains. You can count on a pond or two and a winding dirt road leading to buildings where tours and tastings take place. Typical wooden tasting rooms have plenty of glass so you can look out on the mountains and pond. In cold weather, you may find a fireplace burning with delicious-smelling wood.

For someone who loves mountain views and likes to eat and drink wine, this is the perfect weekend, or an easy day trip. It's not much farther than driving to some of the picnic spots around Washington, and is much more of an escape. The quiet is so great you can hear the wind.

Four wineries are clustered around Front Royal. You can take your pick, or see all four if you are a serious oenophile, though in that case you might want to spend the night because this is not a landscape to be rushed through.

The drive out Interstate 66 becomes less congested and reveals a few distant mountains and roadside farms as soon as you get through Manassas. Oasis Vineyard in Hume was one of the first wineries in Virginia and is now one of the larger ones. When Dirgham and Corinne Salahi looked at property in the area, they knew the soil and climate were similar enough to France to support vinifera—"noble grapes" of the European variety rather than French-American hybrids. The neighbors were sure the effort would fail, but the Salahis proved them wrong, and today other nearby wineries plant vinifera, too.

Corinne will take you downstairs for a tour of the wine cellar, 16 feet underground, where the 10-inch-thick cement walls keep the air naturally cool. Oasis specializes in sparkling wine, which the Salahis called champagne until a call from a French inspector reminded them that this is only permitted for sparkling wines from the Champagne region of France. The Salahis do use the same *methode champagnoise*, a labor-intensive process that causes the sediment to be dropped in a block of ice, which must be removed from the machine by hand, one at a time. It might be easier to do as Dom Perignon did, drinking from a silver goblet so the sediment is invisible.

You can gaze out at the Blue Ridge and the ponds on the property while picnicking at the tables or in the tasting room, depending on the weather. The tasting room has a large stone fireplace that would look at home in a medieval manor. Most years in May, Oasis hosts a festival that includes a cork hunt and the crowning of the Lord and Lady of the Manor.

The drive between the wineries in this area is up and down very hilly roads, past farms populated by Angus cows and bordered by wooden fences. You get to Linden Vineyards, in Linden, by way of Fiery Run Road, driving over a very bumpy slatted wooden bridge. When we were there, owners Jim and Peggy Law had the day off and we made the delightful acquaintance of Andy Pearcy, one of the vineyard managers. Andy clearly loves being outdoors, learning about wine, and sharing his knowledge with all who will listen. He answered our questions and spoke with enthusiasm about the Bordeaux symposium he had attended in Richmond the month before.

You can learn about the bladder press inside the stainless steel tanks, in which the bladder inflates with air, eliminating the grape pulp and seeds. The grape skins are used as manure.

The wines made in stainless steel tanks are clean, crisp varieties—Seyval, Sauvignon Blanc, Riesling. They are only aged 8-10 months, while Chardonnay is fermented in small oak barrels for 11 months and in bottles for a year (that's why it's more expensive). Andy tried to explain the molecular structure of red wine grapes, but ended by saying, "Young tannins grab your glands." Somehow, that says it.

Just 15 minutes away from Linden is Naked Mountain Vineyard, in Markham. This may be the most beautiful view of all: the mountains are close, the ponds are large, the drive from the entrance is winding and delightful. From the parking lot, you can see horses walking calmly through the wooded hills in back of the winery. When you walk into the tasting room, you will be greeted by an old black lab, donated by the animal shelter after owners Bob and Phoebe Harper arranged a benefit. "He runs the place," Mr. Harper says cheerfully.

The Harpers have a machine that is a bit of a phenomenon in the local wine world: a bottling/labeling/corking/capsuling machine. It makes the rounds of different wineries, just the way farmers used to pool their resources and share a threshing machine. Before the machine, it took 2 weeks to bottle a vintage; now this can be done in a day.

Farfelu Vineyard, in Flint Hill, is a small winery being revitalized. Daily tours are available between 11 A.M. and 5 P.M., but call first to check: (703) 364-2930.

If the weather or your appetite dictates more of a meal than a picnic, try Four and Twenty Blackbirds in Flint Hill. This is a small, cheery restaurant in a restored 1860s farmhouse, with polished wood floors, flowered wallpaper, and stone walls in the downstairs room. It serves lunch and dinner Wednesday through Saturday, and a Sunday brunch.

Or, go up the street to the Flint Hill Public House, run by Conrad Koneczny, who had a wine wholesale business in Alexandria before moving to Flint Hill to "relax" by opening a restaurant and bed and breakfast. Sit in the cozy, wood-lined dining room or, in the nice weather, on the deck out back, with its spectacular mountain view. Seats on the deck are reserved a long time in advance in the summer.

You may feel the need for a little exercise after the eating and drinking. Marriott Ranch, just up the road from Oasis Vineyard in Hume, offers Western trail rides through its 4,200 acres. Minimum riding age is 10; beginners are welcome, call (703) 364-2627.

As for me, I'll be back on the deck of a winery, sipping Chardonnay, nibbling on some Virginia gouda, and gazing out over the mountains.

SHENANDOAH NATIONAL PARK

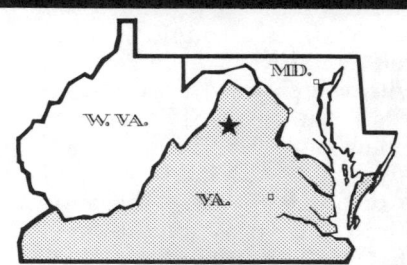

Autumn, of course, is the time for the big show in the Shenandoah. The forests wrap themselves in fiery colors, turning that miracle of unspoiled land, which the state of Virginia presented to the federal government back in 1936, into a breathtaking world. Old Rag Mountain, the oldest rock in the park, shrouds itself in the blue mists of the season and the sneezeweed and witch hazel vie with the late asters for notice. In autumn the Shenandoah is in its finest hour.

But in any season, Shenandoah National Park is spectacular. Covered in winter snow, the park is as primitive and awe-inspiring as undiscovered territory; marching once more to the exuberance of spring, it is alive with the trilling of toads, spring peepers, and returning birds. In summer the park reaches the biological peak of the year, lush with the swamp rose and the bluet, and nursery to newborn mammals.

Interstate 66 is the magic carpet that will spill you out at the park gates behind which deer, bear, fox, and bobcats dwell in this sanctuary, little more than an hour from Washington. Skyline Drive, the 105-mile highway in the clouds that takes you down the spine of the mountain ridge, is one of the wonders of the country. If you drive it in October, at the height of the foliage display, be prepared for bumper-to-bumper traffic. It's not surprising, with the panorama laid out below—the Blue Ridge, the Piedmont, and to the west, the Shenandoah Valley and the Alleghenies. Much of the year, there's a natural pale blue haze over the mountains (don't worry, it's not smog). That's why they're called the Blue Ridge.

What an awesome world lies beyond those ranger gates at Front Royal, the northern entrance to the drive. The city drops away from your consciousness as you climb the steep, winding roads. Deer dart across your path, startled by a noise you do not hear, and halt suddenly to munch the roadside vegetation. If you go in the fall, the valley below is aflame with the reds of sumac and maple, sunshot with the yellows of the tulip poplar and the sassafras. In winter, your journey into the clouds brings you into a world of ice, diamonds coating every branch and sparkling blindingly in the sun. Snowstorms may temporarily close the park, but generally the roads are cleared within a few days.

Shenandoah, once arrived at, is a place for walking. The Fox Hollow trail, just across the road from the Dickey Ridge Visitors Center (the closest to Front Royal), is a couple of miles round trip and offers history as well as nature. You can see the 1916 tombstone of Lemuel Fox (with the chiseled words "Gone but not forgotten by his daughters"), the son of Thomas and Martha Fox, who settled in Fox Hollow more than 150 years ago as tenant farmers. They eventually bought the land, and four generations of Foxes lived there until 1936, when the state moved out more than 400 families to make way for the park. Today, hikers still find pottery from the 1920s around the site of the Fox home. A written trail guide encourages you to wander off the trail and look around, but anything you find must be given to a ranger at the visitors center. Long before this century, Native Americans lived here, but they didn't stay long enough to leave artifacts.

The people you meet on these trails are generally fellow nature lovers, who may tell you in an excited whisper about a deer and her fawn up ahead. This kind of encounter makes it pleasant to meet people in the wilderness.

If you want a longer hike or have specific requirements like a waterfall or a mountain view, just ask at the visitors center. The rangers there are very helpful in answering questions and can recommend trails and give you maps. And when you're ready for a picnic, there's no better spot than the grassy hill behind the Dickey Ridge Visitors Center, looking out at the hazy blue mountains receding into the distance.

As you drive along Skyline, scenic overlooks beckon at every turn with panoramas a billion years in the making. Wind and rain and the upheavals of the earth's crust sculpted these dramatic mountains and valleys from the granite core of the Blue Ridge. Mary's Rock Tunnel, south of Thornton Gap, was formed miles below the earth's surface. A hidden world of interdependent communities of insects, plants, and mammals stretches beneath the tree canopy.

Back in 1894, the rich discovered this kingdom in the clouds when George Greeman Pollock, a wilderness enthusiast and entrepreneur, built Skyland, a lodge to which the elite of the time flocked, though it was so remote they had to get their mail by donkey. Pollock had a flamboyant personality and insisted on arousing his guests with a trumpet blast, but they loved the life and returned season after season. Pollock and his guests are gone with the era now, but his resort is still there, franchised out by the park, with rooms rented to travelers.

Skyland is nice. It retains the feel of rustic grandeur; its fireplaces, burning most of the time, are huge enough to walk into. Outside the picture window in the dining room the Appalachian Trail meanders by, and the view is gorgeous. Your food, with emphasis on southern favorites like ham and fried chicken, is apt to be served by friendly college students on vacation. Check the gift shop for attractive local crafts. Call ahead to check how late in the fall Skyland is open. Its operation comes out of the National Park Service budget, so "it depends a lot on what the congressmen do," a park ranger said.

Byrd Visitors Center, about 45 miles south of Dickey Ridge, has a 20-minute video on the history of the park and rotating displays on topics like park history or wildflowers found along the trails. All the visitors centers have good bookstores that offer everything from trail guides, to histories of the mountain people who were here before the park, to coffee table photo books.

Seeing deer is not at all unusual in the park. In fact, in some areas, deer are fenced out on purpose to make room for other animals. The black bear have returned from the West, where a few had survived the orders of General Philip Sheridan to scorch the earth and cut the trees during the Civil War. The turkeys have returned, expanding up from the south and throughout the park. Recently, peregrine falcons, gradually wiped out east of the Mississippi over the last 50 years, were introduced to the park from the West. So far, 34 falcons have been successfully raised and released into the wild in the park. And once, driving back just as it was turning dark, we caught a bobcat in the headlights.

You can get recorded information about the park at (703) 999-2266. To make lodging reservations, call (800) 999-4714 or (703) 743-5108.

SKYLINE CAVERNS

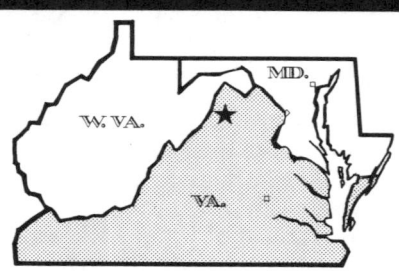

Shenandoah National Park is all you need for an adventure in the clouds, but sometimes, especially if you stay the weekend, the heart yearns for smaller confines, for less grand scenery as a change of pace. This is the moment to see Skyline Caverns and Sperryville, a subterranean world and a small village that package nicely on a country day trip from Washington. Your jumping off point is Front Royal, Virginia, largely known to the world as the northern gateway to the Skyline Drive.

Skyline Caverns, at 60 million years old a Johnny-come-lately compared with Luray Caverns, lies one mile south of Front Royal on Route 340. They were discovered by Dr. Walter S. Amos in 1937, when he and several geologists were exploring the area. The caverns' main attraction is the anthodites, mineral flowerlike clusters that cling to the roof in a special chamber and are seen in only two other places in the world. But the fun is in the tour you get, the guide's patter, the kitsch performance with colored lights and organ music, and the enthusiasm with which you are guided around Dr. Amos's wonderland.

When I last saw Skyline, my guide was a young man who brightened my day with his spiel, and the best thing that could happen is that you also be so lucky. In an accent rich with the twang of the Virginia hill country, he instructed us in the pleasures of his underground domain, shepherding us through like a combined benevolent pedagogue and circus barker. Could we not see that the Capitol Dome formation also brought to mind an elephant's foot stuck in bubble gum? At one point, we were asked to raised our hands if we had no imagination, and the others in the group were asked to help those poor souls out. Then, our guide pointed to a rock formation depicting Mary holding the Holy Child, Joseph, the three wise men, and the shepherds. He said solemnly, "And the amazing part is, this was formed 7,000 years before Christ."

At Mirror Lake, we were asked to guess how deep the lake was. The guesses, ranging from 3 to 19 inches, were all too deep; it's only 2 inches. It looks deeper because you look into it and see the reflection of the stalactites above in the water. A little farther on, we learned that Fairyland Lake has that name because you can see in it whatever you want. It is only 1½ inches at its deepest point, but because of the reflections in the clear water, you can see (our guide told us) two frogs lying on their backs, watching the moon. He made us all ooh and aah in chorus because it's so pretty—hokey, perhaps, but done with such infectious cheerfulness that it's hard to resist.

The anthodites hang from the ceiling in a special room, looking quite beautiful, like spiny coral. They grow an inch every 7,000 years and are said to be 120,000 years old. We don't know how they got here; every theory has been disproven, our guide said with satisfaction, and many geologists have come here to study them. He clearly adhered more to the religious-figures-in-stone school. He shone white, blue, red, and green lights on the anthodites in succession, then turned off the lights and said, "This is the darkest dark you will ever see. Wave your hand in front of your face." It was quite invisible.

Your mile-long walk below the earth's surface is cool—54 degrees year-round—so wear warm clothes. You cannot just look a little and return quickly to your car, because the lights are snapped out as you pass through the caverns and you are captive for just under an hour. But then, you wouldn't want to miss the performance of God in the Mountains in the Cathedral Room anyway, which is a late climax of the tour.

The Cathedral Room is an impressive natural grotto laced with narrow crevices affording a glimpse of tons of rock overhead, a collection of stalactites hanging above a miniature mesa adorned with odd formations. God in the Mountains is a disembodied voice rising above organ music to caution us all to remember that nature's wonders must not be taken lightly in the advance of civilization. Pink glows appear and disappear.

Tour groups go through every few minutes daily. The last price quoted was $9.00 for adults, $4.00 for children ages 6 to 12, and free for kids under 5, but check by calling (703) 635-4545 or (800) 296-4545.

The nearby town of Strasburg calls itself the antique capital of Virginia, and it does have a nice Emporium—a collection of antique stores, flea markets, and craft shops all under one roof. You'll see everything here, from nice hand-turned pottery (for which Strasburg was originally famous) to real junk in some of the flea markets. The town was called Pot Town after the Civil War because of the large volume of pots produced here, and the Strasburg Potters Guild continues today.

If you want a few miles of scenic driving, head down Skyline Drive about 20 miles, get off at Thornton Gap and pick up Route 211 for the drive home, a pretty twisting road bordered by neatly mowed hayfields, roadside apple and cider stands in season, and a breathtaking panoramic view of the Blue Ridge.

On the way home stop off in Sperryville, a little town near Skyline Drive that also has an antique market and an emporium with some of everything. If you feel overwhelmed by emporiums, try the Faith Mountain Company on Route 1001, which sells American country crafts, dried and fresh herbs, unusual women's clothes, and gourmet food items.

Sperryville calls itself the Little Apple and has an Apple Harvest Celebration every October. Its apples are far better than you can find in the stores around Washington (my favorites are Stayman Winesaps) and you can buy them by the barrel here a lot cheaper than you could at home.

For a real treat, stop a few miles up Route 211 in Washington, Virginia. The Inn at Little Washington is the famous restaurant in this tiny town, but you need reservations way ahead and a small bank loan to finance your meal. Some say the Bleu Rock Inn, (703) 987-3190, is just as good, and a lot less pricey. It's also a country inn on an 80-acre farm, 80 of them devoted to the grapes used for the wines served in the restaurant.

LURAY CAVERNS AND NEW MARKET

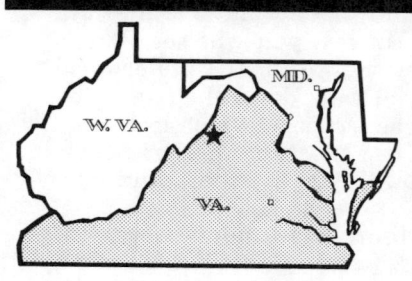

The view from Route 211 winding its leisurely way to the western side of the Shenandoah Mountains makes you catch your breath at every turn. It's an old-fashioned kind of road that encourages dawdling so that you can buy honey and fresh vegetables and savor the pastures and horizons of rural Fauquier and Rappahannock Counties.

The places Route 211 takes you to are nice—Washington, the other Washington in Virginia, where, if you have reservations ahead, you can dine in high-priced style at the Inn at Little Washington; Sperryville, a placid village where antique shops and flea markets lean cheek-to-jowl companionably (the Faith Mountain Company is a good crafts shop); and Luray and New Market, on the other side of the mountain, nestling in the valley.

Luray, the place where in 1878 three young men lowered themselves by a rope into a hole in the ground, is by now, of course, required sightseeing. The caverns put tiny Luray on the map, and well they might, for a journey through these 64 acres where the sun never shines and the temperature is always 54 degrees is like a trip through Frodo's Middle Earth in quest of the ring. Luray has an overpowering assortment of vast natural formations, some as old as 7.5 million years.

It will not surprise you that the caverns were made into a tourist attraction two days after their discovery (the discoverers, three local men, went looking for underground formations for just this purpose). Today, the caverns are part of a large tourist complex with fudge kitchens and souvenir shops. But once you are underground, the commercialism drops off, and it's all worthwhile. True, at the beginning, in the middle of the stalagmites is a large sign warning, "Attendants are authorized to arrest anyone who breaks or defaces these beauties of nature." But after that, except for an occasional joke from your guide about the caverns being insured by Prudential and a piece of the rock, you'll get an informative tour of what is truly one of the natural wonders of the eastern United States.

In case you missed this lesson in high school geology, you will learn how to tell the different between stalactites and stalagmites: Stala*c*tites hold *t*ight to the ceiling whereas stala*g*mites might *g*row to the ceiling. But it will take a while because these rock formations grow only one inch every 120 years.

There's a comment about man and nature in the way people feel obliged to give familiar names to rock formations that are beyond human comprehension. In Luray, you will see Pluto's ghost, a white column named after the god of the underworld that seems to be following you as you walk down the path. One large room has a formation known as Drapery, which looks like a thin sheet frozen in stone, sometimes pleated. Another formation nearby is called the Bath Towel; you'll understand why when you see it.

One of the most impressive sights has a name worthy of sentimental 19th century paintings: Dream Lake. You'll have a hard time believing you're looking at a reflection. Because the water is so clear, you can see a mirror image of the stalactites above reflected in the water. At a depth of 6 inches, the lake would never be deep enough for these formations to be growing from the bottom as stalagmites, though you would swear they were.

Your guide will allow you plenty of time to take pictures—in fact, it's encouraged. One high-ceilinged room is brightly lit so you can shoot without a flash. Everyone on the tour takes turns lining up their family in front of the huge rock formation. But you need to move fast; since the light dries out the rocks, it only stays on for two minutes.

Wear sensible shoes. The tour is an hour long, and sometimes you'll have to step around a stalagmite looming out of the path. You will want to rub the formation that looks like two fried eggs for good luck, and perhaps add a coin to the wishing well that has yielded more than $348,000 of greenish pennies, dimes, and nickels for charity since someone got the idea in 1954.

You might even decide to have your wedding in the room with the stalactite organ; more than 200 couples have. The organ is the caverns' only manmade addition, other than the brick path. In 1957, Leland Sprinkle had the idea of tapping stalagmites with rubber-tipped plungers and amplifying the resulting sound. The organ is mentioned in the *Guiness Book of World Records* as the World's Largest Natural Musical Instrument. Our guide's eyes sparkled as she told us of the wedding where the bride wore a long white train and had to proceed slowly to the underground room as a sheet was laid out for her to walk on, then picked up and laid out again. When the organ isn't playing the Wedding March, you may hear "Oh Shenandoah" or "America the Beautiful."

In the heart of this beautiful valley, just beyond Luray, lies New Market, where on a rainy day in the last year of the Civil War the desperate Confederacy threw a battalion of Virginia

Military Institute cadets into the fight against seasoned Union troops—and won. None of the boys was older than 20 and three were 15, but they managed to capture a cannon and 100 prisoners. Every year on the Sunday before May 15, the Battle of New Market is re-enacted on the site.

Even if you miss the battle, the Hall of Valor, a small, well laid out Civil War museum on the site, will make it all come alive. The building housing the museum is an unusual round structure supported by steel girders. The architect, William Moseley, purposely used weathering steel so its rusty color would resemble blood. Inside, an impressive stained glass window incorporating the names of the dead cadets dominates the hall and the faces of the boys look out from tintypes on the other wall. You keep thinking, as you walk through the museum, how young they were. There's a letter from Beverly Stanard, age 19, to his mother that ends with the words, "And now dear Mother that I may be spared to see you again, and that you may continue in good health will be the nightly prayer of Your darling boy Bev." Next to it is a telegram to the family saying he had been killed in the battle of New Market.

Historians believe General John Breckinridge, who led the young cadets, did not intend to send them into battle. When he ordered them to the battlefield, he said, "God forgive me for giving the order."

Downstairs in the museum, you can see ammo chests, a life-size display of men using a 12-pound cannon, and a model railroad—this was the first major war where railroads played an important role. You can admire the needlework of Eliza Clinedinst Crim, known as the mother of the New Market Corps, a pretty young woman who nursed soldiers on both sides after the battle.

Be sure and see the film that follows the cadets from classroom to battle. It gets around the problem of the war's final victor with the statement, "Who won is unimportant"—although some might dispute that. But the tone has been set, and the narrator continues, "For at least a few hours in the many hours that comprise a man's life, ordinary men were super beings."

Out on the battlefield site, you can look out over the Interstate Highway to the Massanutten Mountains, a small range next to the Shenandoahs. It's oddly peaceful now, as you walk around the Field of Lost Shoes, where the soldiers' boots came off in the mud because the day of the battle was stormy and the wheat fields had just been plowed.

If you are a Civil War buff, you will be interested in the military strategy explained on the guided tour. The tour will also bring you inside the farmhouse of Sarah and Jacob

Bushong, whose family huddled in the basement behind boarded up windows and doors during the battle. There was little damage to the house during the fighting, but afterward it was taken over by Confederate surgeons, who cared for soldiers on both sides.

When you're ready for a break from contemplating man's inhumanity to man, head back toward Luray and drive another 6 miles south to Stanley, where you will find the delightful Jordan Hollow Farm Inn. Its four country dining rooms are between 100 and 200 years old, and the food is much better than the fried chicken that is standard fare elsewhere in these parts. Dinner only is served; prix fixe, and reservations recommended. Call (703) 778-2209 or (703) 778-2285. You can stay at the inn, too, and use their horse or hiking trails, or just sit on the porch and admire the view of the Blue Ridge. This seems like a much better alternative than making the 100-mile drive back to Washington after eating the large and delicious dinner.

A very different place to eat and stay is the Mimslyn Inn in downtown Luray. It is a grand old inn that once hosted Eleanor Roosevelt. You can't miss it as you drive through town—it's an imposing brick building up on a hill, with huge white columns lining the spacious porch. The prices in the dining room are reasonable, and the inn has 49 rooms if you want to make a weekend of it. Call (703) 743-5105.

Luray Caverns is open summer months from 9 A.M. to 7 P.M.; after Labor Day it closes at 6 P.M., and from November 1 to March 15, at 4 P.M. weekdays, 5 P.M. weekends. Call (703) 743-6551.

The New Market Hall of Valor is open daily from 9 A.M. to 5 P.M. except Christmas, Thanksgiving, and New Year's Day. Call (703) 740-3102.

RAPPAHANNOCK RIVER CRUISE

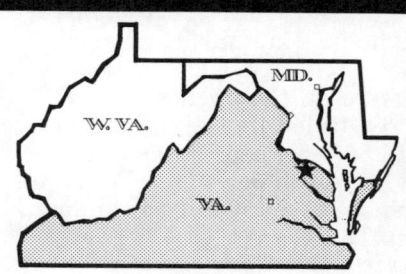

If you love being on the water but don't happen to own your own boat, let me commend to you the *Captain Thomas*. A day on this 70-foot vessel offers some of the delights of Virginia's Northern Neck: bald eagles nesting on cliffs hundreds of millions of years old, a visit to one of the state's largest wineries, and a glimpse into the days when steamboats plied the Rappahannock (before anyone had ever heard of Interstate 95) and area commerce was centered on the water.

It's all arranged and narrated by Captain Tommy Pearson, a Northern Neck native who clearly loves the land where he was born, loves the river, knows boats, and has fun sharing it all with his passengers.

Even getting there is pleasant. You can do it in a day, if you don't mind leaving Washington before 8 in the morning. The only time I've ever enjoyed driving on Interstate-95 was that Sunday morning. At that hour, there's no traffic, the sun is barely up, the sky is big, the horizon low, and as you get closer to your destination, you can find good gospel music on the radio. The last half of your journey, from Fredericksburg to Tappahannock (just remember T for the town of Tappahannock, R for the river Rappahannock) is on Route 17, a nice country road that winds among farms and goes up and down hills, and has signs advertising an asparagus farm and organic popcorn.

It's easy to miss the sign for the cruise when you get to Tappahannock. It's on your left just before you leave town. Park your car, climb onto the boat (don't forget your binoculars, for the eagles), and put yourself in Captain Pearson's hands. He's been working on this boat more than 20 years and will gladly show off its navigational system to anyone interested.

Or you can stay out on the deck and gaze at the sights in the water and on the shore as they drift by. Captain Pearson will fill you in on the things you can't see anymore, like the Adams Floating Theater, which, in the 1920s and 1930s, docked near where the boat takes off. The company rehearsed in the Carolinas, traveled Sunday and Monday, and stayed in each port for 5 days. Captain Pearson's mother and grandfather used to go see the shows.

As you leave the dock, you'll see Frank Perdue's granary, one of the largest grain storage tanks in Virginia. And you'll learn that Hoskins Creek was named after Bartholomew Hoskins—"but I have no idea who he is," Captain Pearson says cheerfully.

It doesn't take long before you're on the open water. You might see a great blue heron, a red-tailed hawk, turkey buzzards, and, depending on the time of year, ospreys or Canada geese. We saw more than 40 bald eagles on our trip, which the captain said was a record (you won't see as many if it's a summer weekend and a lot of boats are out). There was great excitement among the passengers when the first few were spotted. They soar majestically, and the mature ones (age 5 or older) with white heads are especially beautiful. As the captain says, "You don't feel as if you've really seen one until you see the white head." Seagulls follow in the boat's wake for most of the journey, and although they might be considered pests by some, to me there's no lovelier sight than the sun on the water with several seagulls flying above.

You'll pass the remains of a World War I freighter, the *Capunka*; a crab shedding operation; and an old steamboat wharf where a corduroy road was built to provide a way across the marsh. Trees were cut down and their trunks laid side by side—giving the appearance of corduroy—so cars and trucks could drive across it to get to the wharf. The steamboat stopped running in the 1930s, but parts of the road are still in the marsh.

A little farther on you'll pass by Paynes Island Farm, a 750-acre farm that was a gift from King Carter, one of the richest plantation owners in colonial Virginia. At one time, it was a hog farm with more than 900 hogs, but when the land was sold to the current owner, who is more interested in duck hunting, all hogs and hog smells were banished from the island.

Once you leave Paynes Island Farm, you go for several miles without seeing any houses. You pass by Fones Cliffs, formed 355 million years ago. Several sharks' teeth have been found there, which tells us that at one time, this whole part of Virginia was under water. Today, the cliffs are a big feeding area for bald eagles. This part of the journey is pretty and wild—you feel deliciously far from civilization, even though it's only a few miles away.

Captain Pearson is full of useful facts about the passing scenery that you wouldn't know if you were just looking at it—like his revelation that a barn style brick house on shore has a two-lane bowling alley in the second story. A more serious landmark is the house of Hill Wellford, who when we went had just died a couple weeks earlier. He had one of the largest collections of Indian artifacts in Virginia, including some 10,000-year-old arrowheads. When the president of Mexico came to the area a few years ago, Mr. Wellford presented him with several Indian ax heads. Captain Pearson declared Mr. Wellford to be "a good friend of the Bay and a friend of wildlife."

Soon after that is Leedstown, the Northern Neck's answer to the Declaration of Independence. This is where the Leedstown Resolutions were signed, 10 years before the Declaration. Six members of Robert E. Lee's family and five members of George Washington's family were there the first time they decided to stand together as a nation. "When you go looking for the roots of our country, it all started here at Leedstown," the captain tells us.

A couple of hours after you've started, the boat docks at Ingleside winery, just in time for lunch. Captain Pearson, who's sort of a one-man show, drives the bus from the dock and pours the wine at the tasting. On the way, he yells out points of interest such as the plantation house, originally built as a boys school in the 1830s. It was shut down because there weren't enough families willing to pay the $20 tuition. Today, the Flemer family, who owns the plantation, lives there, so it's not open to the public.

You can visit a tiny one-room museum at the winery, where you'll see arrowheads from Mr. Wellford's collection and decoys by local artists. A pretty decent buffet lunch is served in the pavilion, and if it's nice out, you can sit at picnic tables in the courtyard. Some of the Ingleside wines have won several awards, and they make it easy by packing your purchases onto the boat for you.

Mellowed out by food and wine, you can re-dock and bask on the deck until the next step, Wheatland, at Saunders Wharf 27. That means it was the 27th steamboat stop on the Rappahannock from Fredericksburg. You'll be greeted by Fielding Dickinson and his wife Diana. Mr. Dickinson grew up here—his family has lived on the property since before the Civil War—and he still remembers the day the last steamboat, the *Anne Arundel*, stopped at the wharf in 1937. "My father said, 'Take a good look, boy, because you'll never see another one.'"

Mr. Dickinson has restored the old boathouse and made it into a little museum with wonderful old photographs of the steamers, with shots of the impressive state rooms and the saloon, from the Mariners' Museum in Newport News. Although there were 35 stops on the Rappahannock, this is the only wharf that's been restored. The others had flimsy tarpaper tops, Mr. Dickinson says, but this building was kept for other uses through the years; at one point, it was a barn.

During the Civil War, Wheatland was going to be shelled, and Union troops commanded the family to evacuate the premises. Instead, the proud Southern plantation owner John Saunders brought his whole family to stand on the front porch to confront the attackers. He sat in his rocking chair and yelled out, "Damn it, shoot!" (His three granddaughters, all under age 10, later recalled that their knees were shaking with fear.) They were spared; the granary was shelled instead. The family had already hidden the silver under a plank when they heard the Yankees were coming.

If you're interested in seeing the house, you can walk up from the dock, or let Mr. Dickinson drive you in his hay wagon. On the way, be sure to admire the osage-orange tree, which has a 100-foot spread. A member of the U.S. Forest Service was on the cruise one day, noticed the tree, and had it measured—and now it's certified as the largest osage-orange in the United States.

The house itself is a federal farmhouse from the mid-1800s. Mrs. Dickinson, a gracious southern hostess, tells how the steamboats called here three times a week and picked up stock for the stores at Saunders Wharf. Mrs. Dickinson smiles with good breeding and says, "It's hard to imagine all that activity, it's so quiet now—except when the grandchildren are here." After you see the ground floor of the house, she directs you to the garden beyond the gazebo, pronouncing it "gazaybo."

Even though they open their home 6 days a week to scores of strangers, the Dickinsons make you feel welcome. Mr. Dickinson is clearly proud of the boathouse he has restored and the museum he has created, and he'll happily answer your questions, recalling his childhood on the plantation. And when you're done, you have the delightful prospect of another couple of hours on the boat back to Tappahannock, when you can look for more bald eagles or just gaze at the water and daydream.

The *Captain Thomas* leaves Tappahannock at 10 A.M. and returns at 5 P.M. every day except Monday from May through October. At this writing, the cruise costs $18.50 for adults and $9.25 for children under 14. Lunch is $8.95 and $6.95, and the tour of the house and garden at Wheatland is $3.00 and $1.00, for adults and children respectively. Reservations are required; call (804) 453-BOAT.

CHARLOTTESVILLE

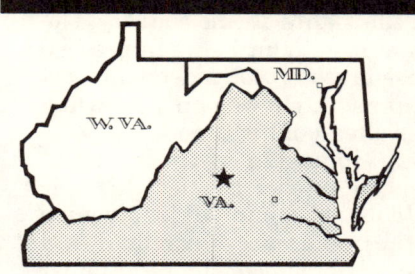

Although I had been warned that Charlottesville is no longer a bucolic southern town, but is as afflicted with rush hour and freeway buildup as the rest of America, my fears melted away as we drove up to our bed and breakfast. A note labeled "Ms. Mooney" was prominently placed on the door. I took it out and read, "Sorry I could not be here. Please come in. Your room is at the top of the stairs on the right. Feel free to watch TV in the sunroom. I look forward to meeting you. Flip Bowers."

I had stayed in places where the hostess has hidden the key while she was upstairs asleep, but never in one where no key was ever used because the door was always unlocked, even at night. Flip Bowers (short for Phillippa), a rare Albemarle County native, was an excellent hostess. When we met her that evening, she offered us a beer and advice about where to eat. Her Cairn terrier, Bear, was a delight, and so was our room, with its lace-canopied four-poster bed. From our window, we looked down on three bird feeders. Her garden, a lovely place to sit in back of the house, was featured in the 1988 Friendly Garden tour. To book yourself into Mrs. Bowers's home or a variety of others, call Charlottesville Guesthouses (804-979-8327) between 12 noon and 5 P.M. Monday through Friday.

Charlottesville has three personalities, and in a weekend you can happily sample whichever you choose. It is famous as the place where Thomas Jefferson and James Monroe built their homes, Monticello and Ash Lawn. Many Washingtonians know it as the home of the University of Virginia (or simply "The University"), which has plenty of history itself but also means Charlottesville is a college town with good bookstores and cafes. The third Charlottesville is least obvious to visitors but can be seen by walking the downtown pedestrian mall or driving out to Duner's for dinner.

Your first stop should be the Thomas Jefferson Visitors Center off Interstate 64. Large and well-marked from town or the highway, the center is open every day, and its employees can tell you about local attractions (including tours of local wineries) and places to stay. The center also sells a block ticket to Monticello, Ash Lawn, and Michie Tavern ($17 at this writing). The block ticket includes a ticket for a tour of the university, which is free anyway—but this reminds you and gives the times of the four daily tours.

Monticello, the remarkable residence Jefferson built atop a hill near Charlottesville, is one of the sights of this country. Nobody could possibly come away from it without being impressed by the genius of this man, who chose law but took a deep interest in architecture, which he taught himself. He was only 26 when he began the house, so full of ideas ahead of his time.

The house, though certainly imposing with its high-ceilinged entryway and 35 rooms, is one of the few historic homes that seems as if it would be a comfortable place to live—perhaps because many of the rooms are hexagonal and have alcoves where beds are stored. Jefferson considered August and September "the sickly season" in Washington, so for all practical purposes the White House was moved to Monticello for those months during the 8 years he was president.

His home is full of his own inventive touches, such as a dumbwaiter from the dining room to the wine cellar, an innovation he brought home from France. You will see a substantial library, but most of the books in it were not his. He donated 6,900 volumes to what later became the Library of Congress, and they traveled to Washington in 10 wagons. The executors of his estate had to sell most of the rest, as the great man died in debt, long before presidential pensions were established.

"All my wishes end where I hope my days will end...at Monticello," he wrote, and it is nice to know that he is buried just down the path from the home he loved. Take the shuttle bus up the steep hill to Monticello, but walk down past the gardens and the vegetable plot to see his grave. It somehow links the past and the present in an impressive way.

The gardens themselves have been restored to the way they looked in the mid-18th century and, like everything else about Monticello, tell us much about Jefferson. He was largely a vegetarian, looking on meat as a condiment in his diet; in the 50 years that followed his first attempt at the 1,000-foot vegetable garden, he experimented with 250 varieties of vegetables and 122 different types of fruit, including many unheard of in other Virginia plantations. His favorite was peas, of which he grew 19 kinds. He was sure that his long life (he lived to be 83) was due to his diet, the product of his gardens.

His position as Minister to the court of Louis XVI in France allowed him to gather unusual seeds, vines, and trees to transplant to his garden, including sesame for salad dressing and the then-unpopular tomato. Patrick Henry scoffed that Jefferson "came home from France so Frenchified that he adjured his native victuals."

In the basement at Monticello we found a display dealing with the current archeological efforts to learn about the life of Jefferson's artisans and slaves. You can see the room the cook lived in, a stark cell 10-by-14 feet.

On your way up the hill to Ash Lawn, stop at Simeon Farm Market, a tiny store in an old stone building where you can get sandwiches and local wine for a picnic (except Sunday, when it's closed). There are picnic tables at Ash Lawn just outside the grounds, so if you've already used your ticket the previous day, you can enjoy the view and a picnic without paying admission again. When you drive in, you will be greeted by peacocks donated by the National Zoo (you can even feed them with peacock food from the gift shop for 25 cents).

While Jefferson inherited Monticello when he was 14, Monroe bought Ash Lawn's 1,000 acres (called Highland then) for $1,000, partly to be near his friend Jefferson. He grew tobacco, corn, and wheat and tried wine grapes, but they were "small and bitter and about the size of birdshot," according to one visitor.

Note the large marble bust of Napoleon in the parlor. Although the tradition was that when statesmen signed a treaty (the Louisiana Purchase in this case), they exchanged silhouettes of each other, Napoleon suited his gift to Monroe to his own larger ego.

The dining room is set for a formal dessert, itself two courses: an American dessert with pudding cakes, pound cakes, and preserves, served with wine; followed by a "light" English dessert of figs, Marzipan, and coffee (presumably necessary so you could stay awake long enough to stagger off to bed).

The parlor and dining room may look inviting, but the family often received neighbors in the bedroom because it was the only room where the house slave had kept the fire going all night. Monroe had about six house staff and 50 plantation slaves. The house is purposely designed so that grubby work spaces like the kitchen are concealed behind the crest of the hill, not visible from the front.

In the summer, Ash Lawn stages outdoor festivals that, says a sign in the museum entrance, celebrate the cultural life of the Monroe era, with jazz, folk music, puppet shows, dance, and crafts. Leaving aside the question of which jazz musicians we might enjoy from the Monroe era, the idea of listening to Mozart and Gilbert and Sullivan under the stars, surrounded by summer flowers with this stately home for a backdrop, sounds lovely—even if there are peacocks braying in the background. In the intermission, you can think about why both Jefferson and Monroe were unusually tall for their time (over 6 feet) and how they both died in poverty, no thanks for getting the nation launched.

Michie (pronounced Micky) Tavern is worth a stop, but it's not in the same league as the other two. For one thing, the tour is by audiotape, complete with rather hokey period music in the background. It has one unusual twist: the 1784 tavern was made into a museum in the 1920s, so it's partly a 1920s interpretation of what tourists wanted to see. Eighteenth century carpenters would never have raised the pegs on the doors, but the 1920s museum owner wanted to make sure tourists saw the nails, so he had them raised. The antique collector who bought the tavern in 1927 moved it piece by piece 17 miles to its present site.

In the 18th century, a tavern was a lot more than a place to drink; it also served as post office, schoolroom, dance hall, and place of worship. The ballroom upstairs at this tavern was the social center of the countryside. Legend has it that Thomas Jefferson's daughter introduced the waltz to America there after she learned it in Paris.

Don't miss the card press, used to straighten out bent playing cards, and the old tavern pipe, provided by the tavernkeeper for guests. Each user would break off a piece of the long stem to leave it clean for the next patron.

If you want to try colonial food, $8.75 will buy you a buffet at the tavern, with black-eyed peas, curd cheese, stewed tomatoes, fried chicken, and homemade biscuits. At the gift shop inside the grist mill at the other end of the parking lot, you can buy souvenirs of colonial Virginia and some of the local wines.

Both Jefferson and Monroe tried to grow wine grapes without success, but a couple of centuries later, the idea has caught on better—there's even a Jeffersonian Wine Grape Growers Society for the many area wineries. The closest to Charlottesville is Oakencroft, northwest on Route 654. You can take a tour of the winery, buy a bottle, spread a picnic, and admire the magnificent view, overlooking a large lake on one side and the Blue Ridge Mountains on the other. Try the Chardonnay, served at the Clintons' first state dinner.

Mr. Jefferson's university has a mystique all its own. It even has its own language: "the lawn," not the quad; "the grounds," not the campus. And its founder is properly referred to as "Mr. Jefferson," not a flip 20th century "Jefferson" or, heaven forbid, "TJ."

Mr. Jefferson founded the university not just because education was his passion, but because he was concerned that so many Virginians were attending northern universities. It opened in 1826 when he was 81, and it had some growing pains. During the first 25 years, when admission requirements were waived, the students were not always the cream of the crop. One member of the Board of Visitors, Joseph C. Cabell, wrote that he was "particularly anxious to be informed on the best mode of governing a large mass of students without the use of the bayonet." That first year, Edgar Allan Poe attended classes for one term before gambling debts forced him to leave.

Charlottesville is proud of its downtown pedestrian mall, where renovations started in the 1970s and aren't finished yet. It's a pleasant place to wander on a summer evening, with a leisurely small town southern feel to it. Be sure and stop at the Old Hardware Store restaurant. Behind the bar, it still has high shelves reachable by sliding ladder, stocked with boxes of Burpee seeds and Westinghouse light bulbs. You can get burgers, sandwiches, drinks, and desserts. It's closed Sunday.

Our other favorite places to eat were Martha's Cafe and Duner's. Martha's Cafe is near the Corner, the student-populated area of shops and restaurants on West Main Street between 14th Street and Elliewood Avenue. It's a very small, reasonably priced restaurant in a house, and is accommodating to vegetarians. The menu changes; when we were there, it had a New Orleans influence. My favorite touch was in the bathroom, where several large goldfish were swimming in the bathtub. Martha's takes checks but no credit cards.

Duner's is on Ivy Road, 5 miles out of town on Route 250 in Ivy. A local favorite, this cheerful country restaurant offers good seafood, beef, exotic egg dishes for weekend brunch, and delicious desserts (try the pecan-chocolate-bourbon pie). More expensive than Martha's but very good food.

The C&O, at 515 East Water Street, has a French bistro downstairs and an elegant, more expensive dining room upstairs; the food is reputed to be good. The Blue Ridge Brewing Co., 709 West Main Street, was started by William Faulkner's two grandsons, who brew their own beer. The food ranges from hamburgers and pizza to more substantial fare.

JAMES RIVER PLANTATIONS

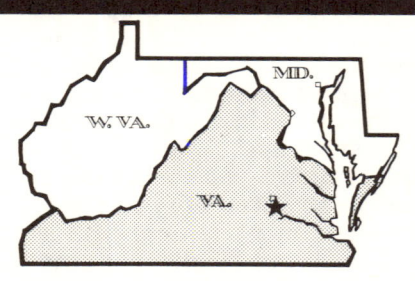

If you think people in Manassas and New Market, Virginia, have not forgotten the Civil War, wait until you get to the James River plantations east of Richmond. Here, the wound from the War Between the States is as fresh as if it were yesterday. They are proud of their heritage and still angry over the way Union troops trampled on it. Visiting Virginia's plantations is fun for a lot of reasons. It's a mecca for anyone interested in old American homes and antiques. If you're a Civil War buff (especially one with southern sympathies), you'll feel right at home. Even if you're just interested in history, it's a bit of a thrill to visit the room where our nation's ninth president wrote his inaugural address or the spot where J.E.B. Stuart fired on Union troops.

And the grounds at all the plantations are beautiful. If you feel surfeited with colonial history, you can enjoy some planned nature among the boxwood gardens and crepe myrtle. Many of the plantations have thoughtfully provided benches facing their impressive view of the river—take advantage of the seats provided. This is the South, after all, and rushing would be out of place.

At some of the plantations, the owners are in residence—in most cases, descendants of the original owners. But things are different in the 20th century: Inheritance taxes are high, farm help is expensive, and if you meet a plantation owner, he's more likely to be a farmer who's been working hard out in the fields than a member of the idle rich.

Several plantations are open to the public along Route 5, within easy driving distance of Richmond and Williamsburg. A good selection to visit is Shirley, Berkeley, and Evelynton.

Shirley has the distinction of being Virginia's oldest plantation. The original land grant for 8,000 acres was given in 1613 by King James I, and the property has been occupied continuously since the 1730s. Like most, it was a tobacco plantation. Tobacco made a lot of money for a few people for a short time, but it depleted the soil quickly. By 1816, Shirley had switched to grain, still grown there today—wheat, corn, and soybeans—on the 800 acres left of the original grant.

Shirley was a center of hospitality in colonial times, when the Hills and the Carters entertained the Byrds, the Harrisons, the Washingtons, Jefferson, and other prominent Virginians. Charles Carter's daughter Anne married Revolutionary War hero Lighthorse Harry Lee at Shirley, and their son was the favorite hero of southerners past and present, Robert E. Lee.

When Charles Carter died in 1804, he designated his grandson Hill (Hill's father had already died) as heir of the estate when he should come of age. But for 12 years, Hill's uncles managed Shirley, and very badly. The family went into debt and had to start selling off the furniture. During the War of 1812, they heard the government was buying lead for bullets, so they sold off bits of the roof. When at last Hill took over the estate, he set to work restoring the plantation.

Today, Shirley's private upstairs quarters are the residence of Hill's great-grandson, Charles Hill Carter, his wife Helle, and their adult son Charles, who will inherit Shirley.

Shirley has cleverly solved the problem of visitors having to wait around for the next tour to begin by allowing you to join the tour group in whatever room is currently being explained, and then to continue on until you have seen all the rooms. Nothing in any of the rooms is roped off, which does give the pleasant illusion that you have been invited around for tea.

The tour of the house starts at the imposing square ring hanging staircase in the front hall. Although it is three stories high, the staircase has no visible means of support, floating up to the current Carters' living quarters. The steps are hollow and actually bounce when walked on. They may sound odd and look strange, but they work: The staircase has been in use since the 1730s and has never needed major repairs.

You can learn a lot from the stories behind the portraits at Shirley. John Carter, whose painting hangs in the parlor, was a lawyer, but he made his (considerable) fortune importing slaves. The records tell us he died of "dropsy of the belly," which historians suspect may have been cirrhosis of the liver. Plantation owners were known for their prodigious consumption of alcohol, and it would not be unusual for one-third of Carter's daily caloric intake to come from liquor.

Something seems not quite right about the portraits of Anne and Elizabeth, two of Hill Carter's daughters from the Victorian era—until you realize they have no upper lips. (This look, known as a rosebud smile, came from Queen Victoria, who herself had thin lips and declared that they were a sign of nobility.) The young women had the portraits painted before they went to England and discovered how unfashionable thick lips were. When they came back they paid the portraitist to paint out their upper lips.

You get a real sense of a living family history at Shirley, if at times an eccentric one. Elizabeth Carter was given an engagement party in the dining room in the 1760s and she wanted to make sure the diamond given her by her suitor William Byrd III was real. You can still see where she scratched her married name, E W Byrd, on the window glass with her engagement ring to test the quality of the stone. Not much of a romantic, Miss Carter, but she did start a family tradition, and you can see other initials in the windows from later brides-to-be.

One of the odder Carter family heirlooms is sitting in the middle of the dining room table, a silver bowl called Nestor's cup, made for a racehorse of that name. Every time the horse won a race, Charles Carter bought one bottle of champagne for himself and one for the horse, and poured them both in the silver bowl so they could drink together.

Most plantation tours don't go into the lives of the slaves who made it all possible, but Shirley provides a small glimpse. Charles Carter had 23 children by his two wives, 13 of whom lived to adulthood. With a brood that size, he often had as many as 45 people staying on the property and eating three meals a day. Because no room in the house is large enough to serve that many, they ate in three shifts, and a good number of Carter's 200 slaves were kept busy. No sooner had they finished the last shift of breakfast than they had to start the first serving of lunch. The kitchen was outside because of fear of fire, so to keep from having to bring dirty dishes across the grounds to the kitchen to be washed, a 100-gallon reservoir was installed on the third floor above the parlor. The slaves had to carry water up three flights to wash the dishes.

After you have toured the house at Shirley, you can sit and contemplate the vicissitudes of history on a bench under a huge old willow oak tree with a span of nearly 75 feet. You look out on a serene expanse of the James River with the sun sparkling on it, wind chimes blowing behind you—though, alas, you can't quite forget the 20th century, with a big industrial plant square across the water.

On the way out, stop and get a brownie and lemonade at Colonel Hill's Extraordinary. A tiny cafe in the old stone kitchen that was used by the plantation until 1941, it has a sort of 1950s decor, with old candy and cracker tins on the shelf and a digital clock powered by a couple of lemons.

As we were getting into our car, a man in grass-stained t-shirt and khakis stopped his tractor and yelled at us, "Did you have any questions about anything?" One of us did, so we stopped to chat. It turned out to be Hill Carter, Shirley's current owner and the 10th generation to live on the plantation. He pronounced Hill like "Heel," with two syllables. We had learned from one of the guides that he only has a couple of field workers to help him.

Clearly, being a plantation owner is no longer the road to riches and a life of ease. A sociable ex-Marine who studied agriculture at VMI and still has a military crew cut, Mr. Carter seems accustomed to answering questions about how he likes living in a house on public display. "It's interesting," he says carefully. "I get to meet lots of researchers and genealogists and historians. But," he adds, "earlier today I had to wait for a couple of tourists to go through before I could go up and wash my teeth."

You won't find any late-generation plantation owners driving tractors at Berkeley, which is a more commercial place. It's quite crowded, complete with an introductory videotape and a well-scripted tour guide. Still, the grounds are especially beautiful, and Berkeley is the site of many historic firsts.

Each of the first 10 presidents was entertained at Berkeley. The ninth, William Henry Harrison, was born there and came back to write his inaugural address in the same room. (It was too long, though, and soon after he read it for an hour and a quarter in the pouring rain with no hat or coat, he contracted pneumonia and died.) The first "official" Thanksgiving took place here on December 4, 1619, when an overcrowded ship came from Berkeley Castle in England. A plaque marks the invention of whiskey in 1621. The first Indian massacre took place the next year. Southern troops retreated to Berkeley during the Civil War, and in 1861, "Taps" was composed here by Brigadier General Daniel Butterfield (great-grandfather of blues musician Paul Butterfield).

Berkeley came into being in 1691, when the property was acquired by the Harrison family that was to send two sons, William Henry Harrison and Benjamin Harrison, to the White House. A shipyard was established on the site, and the Georgian mansion standing today was built in 1726.

When you tour the house at Berkeley, you get an idea of how grand the plantation must have been in colonial times. Many dances were held in the front hall. The fiddlers were three stories up, but the acoustics were so good you could hear every note down below.

The slaves at Berkeley used the whistling walk tunnel to bring food from the outdoor kitchen to the house, so called because they were supposed to whistle while they walked to show they weren't sampling the food as they brought it. Of course, if a couple of them were bearing the platters, one could whistle and the other could sample.

In 1907, Berkeley was bought by John Jamieson, a Scotsman who had served as a drummer boy in McClellan's army. The place was in terrible disrepair, and he bought the property only for lumber. When his son, current owner Mac Jamieson, bought it to restore the house and grounds, there were only five trees left standing—hard to believe, when it's so beautifully planted today.

From the house, there's a long, lovely walk to the river. The five terraces between the house and the river were created by hand, using an oxcart, in pre-Revolution days. You'll find large gardens filled with boxwood and roses, huge willow trees, and a pleasant, spacious gazebo. Gazing down to the river from that distance, you won't be able to discern that the replica of The Good Ship Margaret, which came from England in 1619, is just a painted plywood facade—ocean waves are painted along the bottom—propped up by some planks. Behind it are steps that enable you to have your picture taken as if you were on the ship. But be glad you weren't; it must have been a terrible journey. Thirty-eight passengers and a crew of eight spent 90 days on the high seas in a vessel just 35 feet long.

If you're ready for lunch, stop at the Coach House Tavern. It has good sandwiches and creative salads, and an unusual selection of beer and wine. If it's Sunday, a roving guitarist in knee breeches plays colonial songs like the one about stingo, an ale so strong it makes lawyers plop their heads on the table and forget to collect their fees (wonder if he knew one of us was a lawyer).

The house at Evelynton, a few miles up the road, dates only from 1935, but the grounds emanate history—that seems to be a requirement for having an address along this part of Route 5. Evelynton was part of William Byrd's Westover Plantation when he bought it in 1688. He named it for his second daughter, and it was to be her dowry. That plan was scotched when she was sent to England at age 15 to be presented at court and found a suitor she liked but whom her father thought unsuitable. Evelyn broke off the engagement, but said she would entertain no other suitors. She came back to Westover, where she died of a broken heart 14 years later. The day she died, her father wrote in his journal, "The old relic has passed away." Evelyn's portrait hangs in the hall at Evelynton.

Since 1847, it has been home to the Ruffin family whose patriarch, Edmund Ruffin, fired the first shot of the Civil War at Fort Sumter. The architect was mindful of the symmetry and balance that were important to colonial man—so much so that one door in the dining room, put there only to complete the symmetry, opens onto a brick wall.

Now Evelynton is a working family farm, where Saunders and Betty Ruffin live. The tour guide is eager to explain that Mr. Ruffin is a humble man who can often be found in the nursery by the gift shop and is sometimes mistaken for the groundskeeper.

Evelynton is a lived-in family home: A huge portrait of

Robert E. Lee by the staircase, painted in 1907, has a small hole in it from the time one of the family's small boys tried to shoot soda cans off the banister with a slingshot. In a more contemporary vein is a recent portrait of Sara Ruffin, now in her 20s, and looking in the painting like Jackie Kennedy. Once when a group of attorneys from a convention in Williamsburg toured the estate, the tour guide received many business cards to pass on to Sara.

The grounds at Evelynton are especially inviting. You can while away the time pleasantly in one of the hammocks, looking out at Herring Creek and the James River, near the spot where J.E.B. Stuart fired his cannons on Union troops in the Battle of Evelynton Heights. Our tour guide, a true Virginia loyalist, says that because General Lee sent no reinforcement, Union forces overran Evelynton. They caused senseless destruction, she tells us, her face as dark with resentment as if it had happened to her family only the week before. Now, it's peaceful and quiet.

To get a real flavor of plantation life, you can stay at Evelynton on weeknights for $145 per night, but you need advance reservations. Breakfast is included, and dinner will be provided for an additional charge, if you arrange it ahead of time. It would be fun to stay on when the gates shut at 5 P.M. and the hoi polloi are shooed out of the parking lot.

Two places for food and rest in plantation country must be highly recommended. At the Indian Fields Tavern, on Route 5 near Evelynton, the food is excellent and the surroundings pleasant. Even on a hot day, you can sit quite comfortably on the screened porch, where big ceiling fans rotate overhead. You can get everything from burgers and sandwiches to seafood with nouvelle cuisine touches.

Several bed and breakfasts are scattered along Route 5, some of them looking like miniature plantation houses. We drove to the end of Route 5, took a 15-minute car ferry across the James, and ended in Surry, where we headed for the delightful Seward House Inn (804-294-3810). This Victorian home is run by two energetic older women and furnished with pieces that were passed down in their families. You can stay in one of the rooms in the house or in the cottage next door, which used to be where one of the women's father, the town doctor, saw his patients. When you arrive, they will serve you iced tea and advise you about dinner (with a little advance notice, they will cook dinner for you, with fresh vegetables and herbs from their garden).

Most of the plantations are open every day and charge $6-$8 for a tour, less if you just want to walk around the grounds. For more information, you can call Shirley at (804) 829-5121, Berkeley at (804) 829-6018, and Evelynton at (800) 473-5075.

WILLIAMSBURG BLACK HISTORY

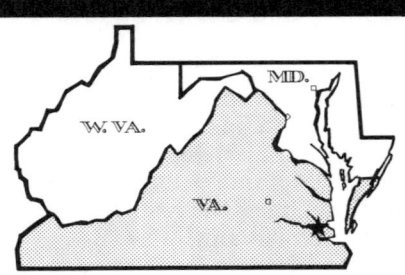

"The Other Half" tour at Colonial Williamsburg is an effort to present a more complete picture of life there in the 18th century. Half the population of Williamsburg then was black—most of them slaves—but until fairly recently, very few blacks were seen working in the historic area. Art Johnson, our tour guide, asks us to adjust our picture of Colonial Williamsburg. "Have you ever been to a city with no poor, no homeless?" he says. We shake our heads. "Imagine them as you walk through Colonial Williamsburg." In the 18th century, most of the people you would see in the street would be blacks running errands or doing chores for their masters.

Yet less than 20 percent of the population owned slaves, and most who did owned only one or two. More than half the white population was made of poor itinerant workers who lived with eight or nine family members in 10-by-12-foot log cabins. So only a tiny minority lived the life you hear about in tours of historic homes and plantations.

The first blacks came from Africa in 1619 to nearby Jamestown, Virginia, as indentured servants. Although both indentured servants and slaves worked at the whim of their masters, there was an important distinction—slaves were property. That meant they couldn't legally marry, so it was all right to separate husband and wife in different households. Such separation was not possible with indentured servants, whose marriages were recognized by the church, because in colonial Williamsburg church and state were the same, and the church declared, "What God hath joined together, let no man put asunder."

Gradually, in the 1600s, the laws of Virginia became harsher toward Africans. One law said that the condition of a mother determines her child's condition—meaning if the mother is an indentured servant or slave, the child automatically becomes one. Another declared that any servant coming from a non-Christian land by boat would be a lifetime servant—a law written to apply only to Africans.

The laws applying to slaves were harsher still. They could not testify in court or bear arms. And if a slave died while being corrected and punished by his master, his owner could go to court and get restitution for lost property.

The importation of blacks really began to pick up in the 1730s, when more than 15,000 Africans arrived in Virginia. On the boats over, the men were chained below deck, while the women and children were unchained above deck. The first time the men were allowed above deck, the boat was already out of sight of land. They panicked, never having been at sea before, and tried to jump off. To prevent this, the slave traders put a net around the ship. The slaves then tried to starve themselves, so the shippers burned the slaves' mouths with hot coals, and when the slaves opened their mouths in pain, they threw food in.

The goal was to make the slaves look saleable once they arrived in America, no matter what diseases they contracted on the way over (dysentery was common). Sometimes this meant corking their orifices to stop them from bleeding, or shaving off all their body hair and oiling them down.

But the slave trade continued, because the colonists had discovered that Africans were ideal for working tobacco plantations. They had already tried shipping over indigent Englishmen to work as indentured servants, but they couldn't handle Virginia's hot, humid climate. Africans were not bothered by the weather; plus, they brought new agricultural methods.

The tour stops at the village green to look at the exterior of the house of George Wythe, who owned several slaves. It was important that house slaves be well dressed and well spoken, since they would answer the door when important personages like Thomas Jefferson and Patrick Henry came to dinner. The most important slave was the cook, not only because cooking in the 18th century was skilled labor, but also because visitors like Messrs. Jefferson and Henry needed to be well fed as they talked of secession. (Slaves' relative usefulness to their masters was reflected in the value put on them. At Wetherburn's Tavern, the most important slave was Caesar, who took care of the horses; he was valued at 75 pounds. The average slave cost 25 to 30 pounds, a year's salary for a journeyman apprentice.)

Most slaves slept where they worked—the cook, for instance, slept in the kitchen. That meant house slaves in the city lived better than much of the white population crowded into log cabins. Field slaves, on the other hand, lived by the theory of out of sight, out of mind (of their masters). Since they were not on public display like the house slaves, they were poorly dressed—they were given clothes twice a year—and usually spoke Creole rather than the King's English. On a plantation, besides house slaves and field slaves, there were skilled craftsmen, such as carpenters, who were even taught how to read and write, to the extent needed for their work.

Another Williamsburg tour, on African American life in the 18th century, takes place in the home of Thomas Everard, deputy clerk for the colony of Virginia and a rich man by 18th century standards. In 1770, he owned a comfortable two-story house and 19 slaves. His footman, butler, and manservant was Bristol, whom Everard had bought from the governor—quite a distinction for the new owner.

Nineteen slaves, says our guide Art Johnson, was not an excessive number for the work that had to be done, such as cooking from scratch. "You ever try to catch a chicken that doesn't want to die?" he asks. Four or five of Mr. Everard's slaves just did the cooking. As in other slave-owning Williamsburg households, most of his slaves were domestics who didn't produce anything, but Mr. Everard still had to support them and pay taxes on them. "That's a major overhead, don't you think?" says Mr. Johnson.

He takes us through the first floor of the house as seen through the eyes of the slaves. In the parlor, we see the remains of "a little genteel gambling" and drinking from the night before. Bristol would have stood along the wall as they played, ready to supply more drinks or fulfill other needs, and Kate and Mary would have cleaned up when the game was over. In the dining room, Bristol put the food on the plates because it was prestigious to have men serve your food, especially a slave who used to belong to the governor. It was the job of the slave children to take out the chamberpots.

Slaves' treatment was largely subject to the mood of their master. "You know how we feel about our pets?" Art Johnson asks us. "That's how they felt about their slaves. I'm not equating slavery with pets, but you want to get into the mindset, that's what you have to do."

A few slaves were able to gain their freedom. They could do this through meritorious service (telling their master of a planned insurrection), through the last will and testament of their dying master, or in some cases by buying their freedom. A slave with a skilled craft like carpentry could be rented out when his master did not need him to build or fix anything, and the carpenter would be able to keep the tips he earned. Field slaves could earn a little money by raising their own chickens and selling the eggs at the market. We know they had their own money because the records show credit was extended to them at the local store.

At Carter's Grove, a plantation a few miles out of town run by the Colonial Williamsburg Foundation, the slave quarters have been reconstructed on the original site using 18th century tools—the only such site in the United States. A good deal of research was done, with help sought from architectural historians and restoration carpenters. Luckily for historians, slaves are talked about a lot in their owners' diaries, with detailed information on how the slave quarters were to be built. On the site now is the foreman's cabin, the smaller carpenter's cabin, and a little house where Sukey and her two children lived with Venus, another female slave.

The slave quarters were discovered by accident. When archeologists excavated the site in the 1970s, they found 13 root cellars and remnants of personal belongings and of a chimney, along with nails, pieces of pottery, textiles, rum flasks, and coins. Some of it is on display in the cabins; much more is in the archives.

As you go into the cabins, the docents in colonial costume outside say, "When you go through the house, don't just say, 'Oh, the poor slaves.' This is how 85 percent of the population lived." It's pretty spartan, and it must have been cold in the winter and hot in the summer. Four to six people lived in each small room—but since there are no doors or windows, the rooms are really more like living spaces. The bed is a thin, torn blanket on a board, or a straw mattress on a rope bed. There's a huge wooden mortar and pestle on the floor and some pottery on a table. There is also what the docent calls "cheap 18th century china," much of it amazingly still whole. It's better than what you might expect—how many people eat off china today?

Most of the slaves' socializing took place in the small courtyard between the cabins. The ground is covered with oyster shells, which were used as gravel. Oysters were plentiful in the James River and were a big part of the 18th century diet. From the time they were born, except in the winter, the slaves walked barefoot on the shells, so their feet soon became like leather.

Carter's Grove was more of a farm than a plantation, with only 200 acres in cultivation. Sixty-five slaves were listed in the 1770 tax rolls, including both house and field slaves. If you've seen any of the other plantations along the James River, you will find this a revealing look at the other side of plantation life. And it will put you in mind of Art Johnson's admonition as you see the other sights of Colonial Williamsburg: "This is how the rich lived."

During the summer, as part of the living history program, you can help Matthew Ashby unload his cart in front of the Prestis Store. Ashby, re-created by a contemporary actor, was the son of a white mother and a slave and was born free in the 1720s. He earned the freedom of his wife and two of his three children by carting goods around Williamsburg. Or you can meet

Gowan Pamphlet, a slave in tavernkeeper Jane Vobe's household who secretly preached sermons in the town. At last check, there were a couple of plays about slave marriage and the disruption of slave households by the impending marriage of their master and mistress, based on the diaries and letters of four 18th century men.

Programs change, so phone (800) HISTORY to check on current presentations. This is a general information number for Colonial Williamsburg. Through it, you can make reservations at any of the inns or restaurants owned by the Colonial Williamsburg Foundation, including four 18th century taverns where you can eat peanut soup and be served by waiters in colonial garb. One warning about restaurants: On weekend nights, they fill up fast, so it is wise to make dinner reservations as soon as you arrive in town. The Trellis, (804) 229-8610, on Merchant Square, serves good contemporary American food. A few minutes outside the historic area is Le Yaca (804) 220-3616, a recommended French restaurant.

CHINCOTEAGUE PONY PENNING

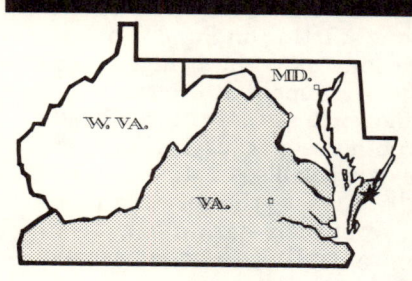

"Sold to the lady over there for $550," intones the auctioneer, "this lovely little palomino filly, maybe a direct descendant of Misty. Take her home and love her. And now, what will you bid, ladies and gentlemen, for...?"

Standing beside the successful bidder, a little girl breaks into tears of joy. She and her sister have been saving for two years for this moment. Now they'll be going back to a little Alabama town with one of the wild pony foals that swam over from Assateague on Pony Penning Day.

It's a story repeated on the last Wednesday and Thursday of July every year, and worth taking a few extra days off to add to your weekend. The small Eastern Shore town of Chincoteague (pop. 3,572) hosts as many as 50,000 visitors who come to see the wild pony herd swim the narrow channel from their island home on Assateague to Chincoteague. And many stay to bid for the little creatures at auction.

The pony penning started in 1925, after two fires in the previous 4 years had destroyed most of the buildings on the island because there was no firefighting equipment except buckets. The Chincoteague Volunteer Fire Company was formed, and the men thought of the area's greatest resource, the wild ponies on Assateague. At that time, the only way to get the ponies across the channel was to swim them, and the firemen held a carnival in conjunction with pony penning day and the pony sale. Then, the ponies were sold for work horses and racehorses; today, they're more likely to go to children brought up on Marguerite Henry's *Misty of Chincoteague*.

As they have every year since 1925 (except the two years during World War II when it was cancelled), all the proceeds go to the fire department—which has ever more beautiful equipment as attendance at the carnival increases year by year. The auctioning of the ponies also keeps the herds down, preventing overpopulation and overgrazing of the grasses on Assateague.

Chincoteague bulges with eager pony viewers for the show, so get out there early, take your field glasses, and face the fact that no matter how soon you get to the shoreline on penning day, there will be hundreds in front of you. The roundup captures the imagination of people from California to New Hampshire, and they'll wait in line for hours to see it.

But here's a tip. The ponies all belong to the Chincoteague Fire Department, which leases grazing rights for them on Assateague. They're rounded up in pens starting on Sunday of that week, so if you drive early Wednesday over the bridge to the refuge on Assateague, you'll see the excitement at the start.

From the Chincoteague shoreline you'll see only horses' heads bobbing in the water. The firemen on horseback, urging them on, will look like toy figures. On Assateague you'll see it all close up—the rounding up of foals too small to swim, the anxious mare whinnying as their foals disappear from their sight into a truck, firemen turned cowboys for the day coiling their ropes and checking their gear. You can talk to the pro cowboys who come in to help the firemen in the roundup, be there when the leader spurs his horse, cracks his whip and yells, "Let 'er go, boys." You can hang over the gate and watch as the herd goes thundering out of the pen.

Fifty-one weeks a year, the ponies lead an idyllic life at Chincoteague Wildlife Refuge, part of the National Seashore Park on Assateague. They roam the beaches, feed on the stubble grass, and drink from the island's brackish pools. Legend says they're descendants of ponies that swam ashore in the 16th century from the wreck of a Spanish ship. The refuge, at the south end of Assateague and at the tip of a great barrier reef reaching down the Delmarva peninsula, is said to be able to support only 150 ponies. Each year the firemen round up and sell off the foals.

Last year, the firemen swam as many ponies as they could, about 150, between a line of boats calculated to keep them from drifting out to sea. With all the money raised at the accompanying two-week carnival each year, the fire company is able to keep a vet on call for the ponies 24 hours a day, giving them worm shots twice a year and checking them over before the swim to make sure they're not too old or too young to make the journey. Pregnant mares are brought to Chincoteague by pony cart.

Chincoteague waits all year for the carnival and makes it into a combination Coney Island-Old Home Week. Snow cones, whirligig rides, hot dogs, fortune tellers, oyster and clam fritters—they're all there. The whole town turns out alongside the tourists and makes a Roman holiday of it at the carnival grounds. The ponies, penned away from the noise and the crowds in the rear, settle down to grazing like old pros after their swim. Some stallions have done it several times.

If the carnival excitement wearies you, drive across the bridge to Assateague, where one of the country's finest beaches awaits you. Assateague's only residents are the ponies, Sika deer, fox squirrels, and various wading and aquatic birds. If you enjoy nature, you'll be delighted with this beautiful refuge. One caveat: Before walking the inviting trails, use insect repellent. The mosquitos are numerous, bold, and big on the marsh-bordered trails.

You'll have to rise early Thursday because the auction starts about 8 A.M. to avoid the heat. The temporary cowboys, volunteer firemen taking a day off from their fishing livelihood, wrestle the foals into a separate pen, and the auctioneer, a Norfolk spellbinder with a rapid-fire spiel, picks up the microphone. Bucking and bracing their front feet against the climb up the ramp, the foals are brought, one by one, to be sold. And ever since Marguerite Henry's story, children from every state have crowded the ring dreaming of owning a foal like Misty.

The auctioneer has the wonderful name of Bernie Pleasants, has been doing this more than a quarter-century, and knows the herds and their history. He likes children and does his best to keep them all happy. Last year one little girl put up her finger to bid every time a pony came on the auction block, but she had less than $500 and never won the bid. When Mr. Pleasants saw this, he talked to a fireman, and when a particular pony came up, he looked at the girl and asked what her bid was. When she told him, he quickly yelled out, "Sold!" The average price is nearly $700, but they have gone for as much as $2,500. Last year, the fire department raised $58,800.

Each time a foal is led off the ramp with a tag around its neck, some child's dreams have come true. Cars start pouring down Route 13 early in the week of the roundup, and more jam the double-lane bridge onto the island before dawn on auction day. Some cars pull pony trailers behind them. One year a family drove from Nova Scotia, pulling the "Pony Express," and went home with two ponies on it.

When the auction's over and cars throng the roads out of town, the firemen put on a sort of miniature rodeo. Any rider who is approved by the pony committee can try riding a wild pony bareback. The object is not to stay on the pony—that's impossible—but to avoid being kicked while falling off. In the early years of the auction, the bronco busting (as it was called then) was performed by ex-slaves.

Several local restaurants open early the day of the auction, and the Masonic Lodge may offer breakfast in different years. Check the local paper, although you'll probably be eating at the carnival at noon, or picnicking. On Saturday, go out by way of Assateague, and stop at the little Oyster Museum before the bridge at the entrance to the wildlife refuge. Here you will find the whole oyster story, as well as delightful period snapshots of earlier pony penning days. You can follow the oyster's progress and see a display of odd articles in which oysters have made their homes.

TANGIER ISLAND

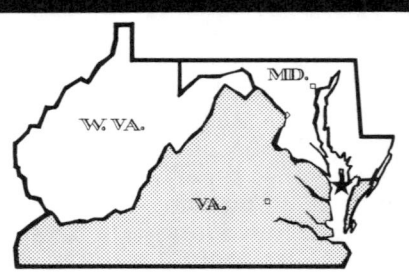

Tangier Island is not for everyone. The accommodations are less than luxurious, the food is fried and fattening, and there isn't much to do. But that's all part of the point. What's most amazing about Tangier, and why it's worth a visit for adventurous urban and suburban types, is simply that a place so isolated exists just a few hours from the nation's capital.

You may have heard somewhere that there's an island in the Chesapeake Bay accessible only by boat, with a population of less than 1,000 who speak in Elizabethan English. Tangier came to the nation's attention with a November 1973 cover story in *National Geographic*. Some enterprising graduate student could learn a lot by studying the effect of the media on Tangier, because that article marked the beginning of a big change in the life of the island. The author, Harold Wheatley, then principal of Tangier Combined School, wrote so movingly about the island where he had grown up that outsiders wanted to visit—and a tourist industry was born.

Captain Rudy Thomas, who ran the daily mailboat from Crisfield, Maryland, to Tangier, decided to start a tourist boat between the same spots, about 15 miles apart. It runs to this day, having passed on to his son when Captain Thomas died a few years ago. The boat ride, lasting an hour and a quarter, is very pleasant—which is good, because if you just go to Tangier for the day, you will spend most of your time on the boat. It leaves at 12:30 noon and returns at 4 P.M., leaving only a couple of hours on the island.

If you're interested in this sort of trip at all, it's worth staying overnight to get more of a feel for the place. Just don't expect to be entertained; there's not even a movie theater. The whole island is only 3½ by 1½ miles, and the inhabited part is quite a bit smaller.

The whole *raison d'etre* for Tangier is crabs. You can get into the mood for this by stopping at Crisfield, which prides itself on being the crab capital of the world. Leaving the port on the *Rudy Thomas*, we heard from the captain that 250,000 bushels of crabs a year come from Crisfield. Looking out over the boat rails, you can see several crab processing plants, and some crabbing boats from Tangier bringing in their catch.

The day we took the boat, there were two bus tours on board, so it was packed. Even so, on a hot summer day there's nothing like a slow cruise out over the water, leaning over the deck to catch the breeze, watching the land recede, looking for an osprey's nest on top of a buoy. Toward the end of the trip, the captain tells you when you're crossing from Maryland into Virginia and from the bay into Tangier Sound. He will also point out a couple of islands bought many years ago by a Philadelphia businessman, who was offered $2 million for one by a developer, but instead donated them to the Chesapeake Bay Foundation. "He gave it away," the captain says, and it's hard to tell whether he's expressing amazement or admiration. But we're all glad the island now has a bird observatory instead of condos.

As you come in to Tangier, you see crab shanties, crab pots piled on the docks, and the spire of the Methodist church—all potent symbols of the island. Tangier now has a population of only 650, down from 800 only in the last few years, and just about all the families make their living from the water—except the ones headed by women, who live off the tourist trade. Crabbing is a hard life, with a workday that starts at 4 A.M. six or seven days a week, and no backup if the harvest is poor. It seems to be an exclusively male occupation. Tangier is a tradition-bound place, and the role of women is no exception. A woman who wanted to be something other than a teacher or the owner of a gift shop (or homemaker, probably the most common female occupation here) would not be likely to stick around Tangier. Maybe that's one reason why the population keeps dropping.

To say that Tangier's population is homogeneous is an understatement. There are only 10 to 12 surnames on the island, and about three-fourths of the residents are named Crockett, Parks, or Pruitt. There is a single school, with about 135 students from kindergarten to 12th grade, and 10 seniors in the most recent graduating class. The class valedictorian won a scholarship to William and Mary, and it's hard to imagine that he would come back to Tangier after graduation to make a living on the water.

Tangier has none of the amenities of daily life that you take for granted just about anywhere else in America—things we foolishly think of as necessities, from private automobiles to dry cleaners. There is a business center with a copy and fax machine, as a hand-lettered sign by the side of the road informed us. There are only about 12 cars on the island, brought over by barge, and most are used for business. Everyone else uses a moped, golf cart, or one-speed bicycle (that's all you need; the island is nowhere more than 7 feet above sea level). Anyway, the street is not much wider than a single car. There is no doctor living on the island, but one flies in twice a week, and a nurse lives here. (Don't worry; if you fall seriously ill while you are on the island, a helicopter can whisk you off to the mainland.)

Tangier has a sort of schizophrenic relationship with tourists. Especially with the crab harvest as up and down as it has been recently, Tangier residents really need the income brought by summer visitors. And it's not going to make them rich. When we stayed at one of the two inns on the island, the Chesapeake House, each of us paid $40 for the room and a large dinner and breakfast. About the only other money we spent was $2 each for a golf cart tour of the island and $5 to rent a bicycle for the weekend.

And yet, as we rode around in our guided golf cart, gawking and feeling very urban in our styled hair and Smithsonian t-shirts, we caught Tangier residents smiling with bemused tolerance. What must they think of the noisy, staring tourists who can double the island's population as they throng the streets for a few hours? One woman on our tour asked the guide what the median income on the island was. Our guide pretended not to hear her the first time, and when asked again, said, "I don't know. I just know what I make." Luckily, our fellow tourist didn't pursue it further.

You will hear a lot about Chesapeake House if you are visiting the island. It is one of three places to eat and of two places to stay, and has won awards for its food. Be sure to call ahead if you want to stay overnight, since there are only a few rooms. When I called and said I was looking for space for three adults, the woman said, "What sex are y'all? I have a family suite open." Since the price was the same, we waited for a weekend when we could get two rooms. We were told that family-style dinner was served at 5 P.M. Although this was about 5 hours earlier than my usual dinner hour, it left us plenty of time to go to the beach afterward and watch the sunset, go "downtown" for an ice cream cone, and retire to our rooms to play cards before going to bed. On the street, we had to dodge the teenagers, whose big Saturday night activity is to ride around the island on their mopeds. They surely surpassed Tangier's 15 mph speed limit.

Perhaps it is just as well dinner is so early, because if you ate a meal that large and went to bed soon afterward, you might never get up. We had crab cakes, clam fritters, green beans, potato salad, coleslaw, applesauce, ham, beets, corn pudding, bread, iced tea, and lemon cake. It is fun to sit at the long tables and meet new people, although there were so many Washingtonians at our table that I ended up sitting across from someone who lived a few blocks from me at home.

Don't expect to drink even a Bud with dinner. This is Methodist country, and there's no alcohol to be found. You can bring it over on the boat, but you have to be pretty fond of your liquor to want to carry it from the boat to the inn along with your bag.

Besides the Methodist church, there's also an interdenominational one (a sign in its graveyard says, "Private cemetery; no pictures"). On Sunday morning, most of the island is headed for one of the two. By that time, I had slowed down enough to find it quite enjoyable to sit on the front porch of the Chesapeake House, watching the residents go by on foot, bicycle, and moped, dressed up in their Sunday best, on their way to church. I have never seen so many bicyclists in heels.

Sunday morning, when most of the tourists are gone, is also a good time to hear the way the islanders speak among themselves. I'm no expert on Elizabethan accents; this sounded to me like a thick Scottish brogue—practically unintelligible to an outsider. Of course, when speaking to tourists, they sound like any other Marylander. It's like being bilingual.

Tangier has a lovely bayside beach, facing west so you can watch the sunset over the water, not an easy thing to do on the east coast. It's an easy bike ride or a not very long walk. If it's a nice day, you'll find several bikes waiting on the marsh grass, none of them locked. Where could a bike thief take the stolen goods?

Be sure to bring bug repellent and sunblock to the beach. There's no shade and plenty of mosquitoes and horse flies, especially when you have to pass through marshland to get to the water. The minute the sun starts to go down, the bugs come out in force; even the screened porch at the Chesapeake House couldn't keep them out.

And of course, swimming in the bay means you risk bumping into jellyfish. When we were there, it was so hot that I threw caution to the winds and jumped in. It felt lovely, I did get stung, it hurt a lot at first, made a bad welt, and went away completely after a few hours. Different people react differently. You can walk a good portion of the island on the beach. In one direction, all you can see is sand, water, and marsh grass; it's lovely and peaceful.

It gives you a tiny feeling of the pull of the water on the people of Tangier. Mr. Wheatley, in his *National Geographic* article, put it eloquently: "There is change on Tangier," he wrote, "but one element of our life never changes: The sea is our highway, our farm, our prison."

What he didn't count on was the lure of the rest of the world. The island has cable now, and kids growing up on Tangier can learn from TV about a life outside that is less harsh and more complicated—perhaps appealingly so. It is hard to know how long a place like Tangier can resist the pull the modern world exerts on its young people. But for now, we can feel grateful that it does exist, and not just because we city folk like crabs.

Chesapeake House is open from April 15 to October 15; call (804) 891-2331. You can also stay at the Sunset Inn, (804) 891-2535, which has balconies that overlook the bay. The *Rudy Thomas* leaves Crisfield (about 3½ hours from Washington) daily from May 15 through October at 12:30 noon; call (410) 968-2338. The rest of the year, you can take the mailboat, which leaves Crisfield at 12:30 and returns at 8 A.M., every day except Sunday. You can also take the *Captain Thomas* from Reedville, Virginia, but must be there for a 10 A.M. departure. Call (804) 333-4656.

MARYLAND

Many Washingtonians, when they think of weekend trips to Maryland, think of Ocean City or, if they have more imagination (I'll state my prejudices up front) of the Chesapeake Bay. And the Chesapeake is one of the best reasons to live in this area. Eating the crabs would be reason enough, but the Bay has a culture and a mystique all its own: the distinctive flat landscape, the osprey nests in the water, the lore of the skipjacks and bugeyes, and the life of that diminishing breed, the watermen.

But, appealing as it is, there is much more to Maryland than the Bay. The Free State offers astonishing variety for a relatively small state, and much of it, amazingly, is fairly undiscovered. To the west is Garrett County, whose mountainous landscape gets more snow in the winter than some parts of Alaska. To the northeast, Ellicott City is a must for railroad buffs and a pleasant place for a little shopping and a nice meal

in a small-town historic district. Havre de Grace has a different kind of small town atmosphere, centered around the Susquehanna River. Or you could go to a winery in Mount Airy or several antique shops in New Market. And don't miss Ladew Topiary Gardens, the Harford County brainchild of a Long Island native who planted these gardens where a unicorn, sea horses, and Churchill's top hat are all carved in the greenery.

Southern Maryland has many undiscovered parts as well. The Western Shore, while gaining in popularity, is more low key than its eastern counterpart. Except in the crowded peak of summer, Solomons Island is a restful spot at the southern tip of the peninsula, with an excellent marine museum.

If you do want a swimming beach, there's none better than Assateague. It makes a nice trip combined with a visit to the nearby towns of Berlin and Snow Hill, where you can eat a gourmet meal at a Victorian hotel and take a nature cruise down the Pocomoke River in a tugboat.

Maryland isn't just for crabs. It's also for anyone who likes rivers, the ocean, the bay, the mountains, ospreys, marine life, small-town parades, harbor views, waterfront dining, early American history, antiques—the list could go on. Try some of these trips and see for yourself.

LADEW TOPIARY GARDENS

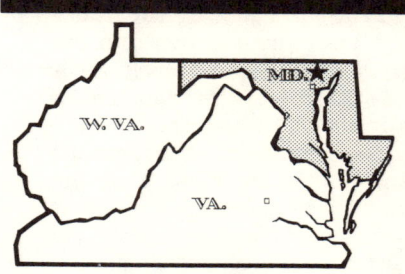

Here comes the fox and now the hounds in hot pursuit, followed by the huntsman on horseback. The hounds will never catch the fox and the horse behind will never land all four feet on the ground. They're all topiary animals formed from green bushes in the gardens of Harvey S. Ladew in Monkton, Maryland.

Harvey Ladew died in 1976 but he left a legacy scarcely to be believed. He was a wag, and his house and gardens, open to the public and administered by a private foundation, are full of jokes and surprises. They are also beautiful.

Ladew grew up in Long Island, but he didn't much care for its wire fences, which he found a hazard to his fox hunting. So he bought Pleasant Valley, an old farmhouse in Harford County near Baltimore. With plenty of cash to indulge his eclectic tastes, he proceeded to make it over, with the help of decorator Billy Baldwin, into one of the most delightful places imaginable. The Garden Club of America awarded Ladew a medal for the most outstanding topiary garden in the country developed without professional help.

Ladew's sense of fun is everywhere. In the apple orchard, he tucked away a statue of Eve offering Adam a piece of the fruit. Around the sundial he had the words of Hilaire Belloc carved:

> I am a sundial and I make a botch
> Of what is done far better by a watch.

The view from an open window in the tea house, once the ticket booth at the London Tivoli theatre, is framed like a landscape painting. Above the doghouse by the front door of the farmhouse is painted an unattributed poem:

> I love this little house because
> It offers after dark
> A pause for rest, a rest for paws
> A place to moor my bark.

It is the topiary, of course, that made him famous, green-growing creatures formed by training living plants into a wire frame and clipping recalcitrant branches. A reindeer complete with antlers watches the front door, a lyre-bird spreads his tail in the sculpture garden beside a unicorn, sea horses, and a replica of Churchill's top hat. There is even a topiary Henry Moore sculpture, the only abstract in the lot. Close by the house lie the terrace gardens, which stretch over three levels and are designed to look like outdoor living rooms. The hemlock walls are clipped into garlands and pyramids, adorned with French hens sitting on nests and cut through with windows to open the view.

What a charmer this Ladew must have been, if one can go by his portrait, wearing his hunting pinks as master of the Elkridge-Harford Hunt. It's easy to imagine the hearts he must have fluttered with his dark good looks and his huge inherited fortune. An only son, he was brought up royally and spent his time with the famous of his day. He was always traveling and once, when Ladew accompanied an expedition to a South American mountain range, a naturalist discovered a new species of mouse and promptly named it after Ladew. Crossing the Arabian desert, he felt the wind, and bedding down with a caravan of Bedouins, wrapped himself in the dinner jacket his uncle had cautioned him to bring.

He had more than a passing acquaintance with royalty, and was particularly close to Edward VIII before and after his abdication. He kept up a lengthy correspondence with Lawrence of Arabia. On the wall of Pleasant Valley hangs a letter from Lawrence lamenting the times. "Everything, everywhere is changing," he wrote to his friend in 1924.

A visit to Ladew's house is a discovery trip into the life and times of the man who owned it. He not only had the money to indulge his whims, but he did it with verve and imagination. He bought a particularly fine oval desk in England and, finding no room in his house big enough for it, built an oval room to accommodate it—a room now said to be one of the 100 most beautiful in America. It's lined with 3,000 volumes of first editions and biographies with a bit of classic erotica thrown in. He had a secret panel added, so that the wall panel swung wide to allow him to disappear into the card room. When he tired of tennis and took up croquet, he brought a part of the net indoors and had it attached to a Sheraton hunt table to catch the empty bottles at the hunt breakfasts.

It all comes off quite splendidly, though Ladew mixed treasures and oddities with a fine disregard for rules. "These rooms are like gardens, and sometimes became unweeded gardens," wrote Billy Baldwin of his friend and employer. The rooms don't look like period museum pieces; they look inventive, and sometimes they shock. His bedroom, for instance, is perfection: an old four-poster, his hunting pinks laid out complete with needlepoint slippers featuring fox heads, a French history on the reading table, and beside the bed an ashtray inscribed, "God bless this lousy apartment."

Bring the children. They will enjoy it all—the mazes in the garden, the fountains, and the game of discovering the hunt motif hidden everywhere. Children love the mantle clock that plays a march, a minuet, and a sonata, and the *trompe l'oeil* painting selected by Ladew for the dressing room his sister Grace used when she visited. The painting takes an entire wall, turning it into a chest of drawers from which dangle bits of intimate feminine wear. Two chairs at each end are also awash with discarded bits of lingerie.

Don't miss the silver dollar embedded in the newel post to signal a paid-up mortgage in 1847, when the former owner lived here. Or the thank-you note from the Prince of Wales after a loan of Ladew's favorite mount, The Ghost. And be sure to look up at the dovecotes in the garden, which are as elegantly designed as any summer cottage.

Harvey Ladew liked things nice.

ELLICOTT CITY

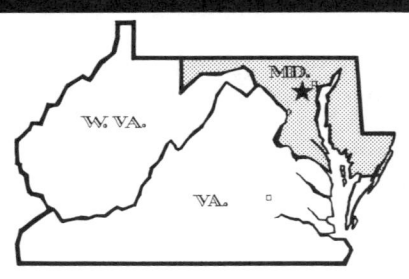

Back in 1830, a gallant gray horse pulling a stagecoach toward Baltimore from Relay, Maryland, was losing a race with one of the new Iron Horses of the railroads when a band slipped from the drum of the little Tom Thumb engine. The gallant gray pulled ahead to win. But it was one of the last victories for horseflesh in the age of steam. In Ellicott City, Maryland, they still remember the day.

Ellicott City is no longer the sleepy country town it was 10 years ago. The population has quadrupled, and many of the residents now commute to Baltimore. But it's still a charming town, full of carefully preserved history, with several nice restaurants and shops along Main Street. It was built more than 220 years ago, high above the Patapsco River on land belonging to three Quaker brothers named Ellicott. At the end of Main Street sits the first railroad terminus in the United States, an old stone edifice now declared a National Historic Landmark.

"I consider this among the most important acts of my life, second only to the signing of the Declaration of Independence, if second even to that," said Charles Carroll as he laid the cornerstone for the railroad in 1828. You can learn about the railroad's early history at the B&O Railroad Station Museum, next to the tracks at the end of town that are still used by CSX to transport cargo. When the granite stone station was built, it was the end of the B&O line for the 13 miles of track between Baltimore and Ellicott's Mills.

An elaborate model of those 13 miles can be found upstairs in the freight house. This must have been quite an undertaking for the 30 people who built it, constructing many of the miniature buildings along the tracks from scratch, using old photographs. Along with the Ellicott City Depot and the Avalon Iron Works, you'll see the Patapsco Hotel, where railroad passengers stayed in the 1830s and 1840s. Henry Clay is said to have spoken to a crowd gathered below his window while he stayed there. Later, the hotel became the unofficial Union headquarters during the Civil War.

Just outside the freight house is the turntable pit used to turn locomotives for their run back to Baltimore. It was uncovered by Catonsville Community College students in 1974, but with funding being low, it's now so overgrown you can hardly see it. When a little more money comes in, the museum hopes to put a reproduction of a railroad car in the pit.

On the first floor of the museum, you can see a freight agent's office and quarters, circa 1831. The water supply had to be retrieved daily, so he got by on one or two buckets a day. His food was mostly dried or cured. It was a pretty spartan existence, with his only diversion a game of solitaire and a few puffs on his pipe before retiring to his cot.

Upstairs is the office of the Superintendent of Construction, Casper Weaver, who in the 1830s supervised the building of a branch line from Washington to Ellicott City. When President Andrew Jackson came here by stagecoach in 1833 and used the B&O line to continue to Baltimore, he was the first U.S. president to travel by rail.

During the Civil War, thousands of Union and Confederate prisoners passed through this station. Now, every couple of months the Patapsco Guards, re-created Civil War troops, are there in uniform, with their muskets. When I was there, an officer was demonstrating how to clean a musket and showing what a different sound it made when clean. He explained that a soldier who had been found to have a dirty musket was going to have to stand guard duty as punishment.

At the other end of Main Street, be sure to see the Howard County Courthouse, built in 1842 on top of Capitoline Hill, sometimes known as Mount Misery. The original courthouse was built on Main Street, and the barristers had to shout over the sounds of the cows, horses, and goats being driven to market on the Frederick Road—as well as endure their smell. They also had to put up with periodic flooding from the Patapsco. All this made it seem like a good idea to build the new courthouse on the hill.

The way there is steep and winding and can be reached by car, or for the energetic, on foot. (It's not far from Main Street, just high.) On the way, there is a private home with set after set of steps leading up from the road to the front door; you can only hope there's level ground in the back for bringing in groceries.

The courthouse itself, still in use and recently renovated, has quite an impressive dome. A stone building at the rear, built in 1840 for the Edwin Parsons Hayden family, has beautiful wrought ironwork on the first and second story porches, reminiscent of New Orleans. When the Howard County District Court used the building for offices in more recent times, court workers used to swear they smelled breakfast cooking when they came to work, although the house has no kitchen. Apparently the Hayden family spirits lived on in the house, sometimes turning doorknobs and making floors creak.

Across the street from the courthouse is a little stone and brick alcove with a picnic table in it, sheltered by a large tree. This is a lovely place to look down on Ellicott City's back streets while enjoying your picnic, or just resting your feet after the climb. You can look across the river to Baltimore County.

Next to the picnic table is a small museum run by the Howard County Historical Society, open 1 P.M. to 4 P.M. Tuesday and Saturday. It has a permanent exhibit of Howard County furniture, and rotating exhibits of everything from teddy bears to bridal gowns (black gowns, it turns out, were fashionable in the 18th and 19th centuries).

When you've seen the courthouse, go back down to Main Street and stroll past the shops and old buildings. You can pick up a walking tour of the historic district in several of the shops. Take the advice of Grace H. Sherwood, who wrote in 1926 in the *Baltimore Sun* that a visitor to Ellicott City "must go to her reverently on foot. She will not reveal herself to the hasty and the superficial, because haste and superficiality have had no part in the fashioning of her."

The town was originally called Ellicott's Mills, after the Ellicott brothers—Joseph, Andrew, and John. Paying $3.00 an acre for 700 acres and water rights, they built a mill to produce plaster of Paris, which was found to fertilize soil depleted by tobacco so it could grow grain. The Ellicotts milled wheat and other grains in additional mills. The original mills burned around 1805, and their replacements were destroyed, like much else in the town, in the flood of 1868. Fifty people died in that flood, and many residences were wiped out, along with railroad tracks, bridges, and places of industry along the Patapsco River.

The damage was said to be even worse when Hurricane Agnes swept through the town in June 1972. The old stone house of Jonathan Ellicott, Andrew's son, was washed away and buildings on Main Street were submerged almost to Columbia Pike.

Although many of the town's early structures were destroyed by flood, you can see the town's first fire station, built in 1896 and now a museum. The bell in the cupola was rung when volunteers were needed to form a fire brigade. A two-story building had been planned, but only $500 was raised, so the fire company made do with a single story.

Now, Main Street is a combination of crafts and antique shops and 1960s-style crystal and tarot shops. Ellicott Square, at 8167 Main Street, has several shops and a little porch in the back with a bench that looks out on a stream. Be sure and visit

Tusker's on the second floor, which has unusual handmade dolls: an old Jewish immigrant with a full beard, Hebrew bible, and baskets for sale; old black men in suspenders, playing chess; and Indians with full headdress and drums. Farther up the street, Ellicott's Country Store has three floors of antiques, country crafts, and old prints.

When you're ready to eat, try Tersiguel's French Country Restaurant, 8293 Main Street, or Only the Best Restaurant, in Ellicott Square. PJ's Bake Shop and Restaurant and Cacao Lane have outside decks where you can eat if it's a nice day.

Five miles away on Landing Road in Elkridge is the Cider Mill Farm, the last one operating in Howard County. The smell of apples assails you as you get out of your car, and the tone is set when you see a row of little red wagons for hauling children around the farm, propped up against the wall of the store.

The farm has a petting zoo, and it's a great place for kids and city folk of all ages. There's nothing like the rough tongue of a two-month old calf licking you when you pet him. Baby goats eat grass from a little boy's hand, and a small girl calls out triumphantly, "I gave the calf a kiss." A rooster crows, a big pig sleeps happily in the sun, and the bronze turkeys (not for petting because they might nibble your fingers) make sort of a trilling coo. It's all quite peaceful and pleasant, and if you want to stay for a bit, you can seat yourself at a picnic table to enjoy some cider from the shop.

Inside the shop, you can watch a 48-ton cider press at work. It requires two or three people to run it, and it's quite a show. A long pipe runs from the back room (where the apples go in to the press and are chopped) to the front. Tom Owens, the owner, says the secret is to use one type of apple from each of the four major taste groups: in this case, Stayman/Winesap, York, Red Delicious, and Yellow. It seems a professor at Purdue wrote a paper on the subject.

This is Mr. Owens's second career. He was an engineer, but he took a values clarification test and decided farming would make him happier. (He has fond memories of the time he spent as a child on his grandfather's farm.) He's still an engineer in the off-season, which is summer for apples, so the farm is closed to the public then. For more information, call (410) 788-9595 or (202) 775-0696. For general tourist information about Howard County, call (800) 288-TRIP.

HAVRE DE GRACE

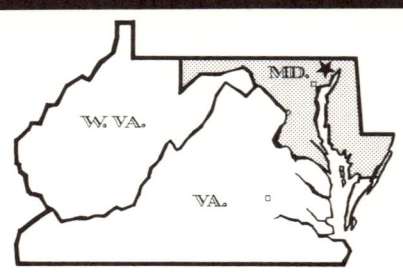

It took Havre de Grace a while to discover its past—up until the Bicentennial, really. In the old days, residents of this pleasant harbor town were called "river rats" and were thought to live on the wrong side of the tracks (literally—Amtrak still runs through the area). This has its advantages. It means you won't find it overrun with tourists. You may not feel you want to swim in the river (though many local children do), but it's pleasant to walk or sit by the water's edge. The view is lovely; you can see both the Susquehanna River and the Chesapeake Bay. Perhaps because they've reached out to tourists relatively recently, the residents of Havre de Grace were among the friendliest I encountered on these trips.

Unfortunately, there's no pleasant way to get to Havre de Grace from Washington, so you might as well go for efficiency and take Interstate 95. When you arrive, it won't be hard to find Union Avenue, the main street. If you come by land, you pretty much have to turn right on it to get to the area that has the Decoy Museum, the lighthouse, and the recently built wooden promenade that connects them. In the works in the same area is a maritime museum and the renovation of the lighthouse keeper's house into a museum.

Park your car by the Decoy Museum, which is sort of a monument to decoy carver R. Madison Mitchell, started by his grandson Mitch Shank and Mitch's mother, Madelyn Shank. Mitchell, who died in 1993 at age 97, was the son of a Havre de Grace milkman who had a funeral parlor and a decoy shop and carved both working and decorative decoys. The decorative ones, of course, have more detail (ducks can't see well enough for the details to be needed on working decoys) and are more expensive. One wall of the museum is taken up by life-size wax figures of Mitchell and two of his hunting and decoy carving cronies, gathered around a pot-belly stove; it's a 3-D re-creation of a 1942 photo. Mitchell never worked a day without wearing a bow tie. You can see it in a photo of him and Governor Schaefer.

Among the display cases of decoys by Mitchell and other carvers is an exhibit on the evolution of the shotgun, just in case you'd forgotten the original purpose of decoys. Somewhat ironically, the museum is working with environmental groups now.

Mitch Shank reports proudly that in the local middle school, the seventh and eighth graders are making decoys in shop class.

Walk out of the museum past the small garden planted with fragrant lavender and go down to the Promenade, a winding boardwalk that leads to a tiny snack bar and snow cone stand on one end (there's nothing like a snow cone on a hot summer day). As you walk along the river, you'll see herons, redwinged blackbirds, and numerous ducks.

At the other end of the Promenade is the Concord Point Lighthouse, the oldest continuously operating lighthouse in the United States. It was manned by the O'Neill family until 1928; now it's automated. John O'Neill was named the first keeper of this lighthouse because of his heroic defense of Havre de Grace against British forces in the War of 1812. He fought them back practically singlehandedly with two small batteries, including one called the Potato Battery. The British captured him, but when his young daughter Matilda pleaded for his release, they relented. The charms of a young girl work wonders, then as now.

Concord Point is where the bay meets the Susquehanna River—which, though you may think of it as a Pennsylvania river, originates in Cooperstown, New York. The view from the top of the lighthouse is impressive, but not for those with a fear of slender ladders or small (and in the summer, very hot) spaces. It does give you an expansive view of the harbor, bay, and river that you can't get from any spot on the ground.

In May, the Decoy Museum holds a festival, with a decoy auction, a head whittling contest (that's decoy heads), a punt gun demonstration, and a duck and goose calling contest. The world of decoys is an entire subculture of its own, often far removed from the original purpose of hunting. You can learn about different paint styles and see who wins the award for best decorative decoy. For information, call (410) 939-3739. The museum has a smaller scale festival the first weekend in May. If you prefer old boats, there's an antique classic boat show in June and a wooden boat expo in July at the Havre de Grace Maritime Museum, next to the lighthouse; call (410) 939-4800.

The Susquehanna Lockhouse Museum at the other end of this town is worth a look, too. Its history is tied up with the water. The museum, at Erie and Conesto Streets, is at the first lock of the Susquehanna River and Tidewater Canal, and is furnished like an 1840 lockhouse. The canal, opened in 1839, provided a vital link between Philadelphia and Baltimore, starting here in Havre de Grace and running 45 miles up to Wrightsville, Pennsylvania. In the early days of the 19th century, lumber had to be brought down from New York by rafts during the annual overflowing of the river, usually in February, March, April, and May. Navigating the river was expensive, not to say dangerous.

The canal was in full swing around 1870. With the canal boat moving about 3 miles per hour and encountering a lock about every 1½ miles, the trip to Pennsylvania took a couple of days. During the Johnstown Flood in 1889, many sections of the canal were washed out and many cargo boats stranded. Maintenance simply became too expensive—especially with competition from the railroads—and the canal closed over the next several years.

The job of the lockhouse keeper, whose house you see here, was to collect tolls, swing the bridge open and shut for boats, open the gates, and keep records for the canal company. It's a fairly comfortable two-story dwelling, close enough to the river to have had its first floor flooded several times—most recently during Hurricane Agnes in 1972. During renovations in the 1970s, architects found five separate foundations under the porch.

The museum is sort of a catch-all for Havre de Grace paraphernalia. My favorite is the telephone switchboard from the 1940s, with its numerous wires that were connected by female operators ("Number, please?"). Before Ma Bell, all long-distance phone calls between north and south had to go through Havre de Grace—even calls from the White House.

Another thing Havre de Grace was known for earlier this century that you won't find commemorated in any museum is the racetrack. Remember *The Sting*, where the characters talk about going to The Graw, as in the Havre de Graw racetrack (an attempt at a French accent, presumably)? The track, on land now owned by the National Guard, was one of the top four or five in Maryland, back when there were several to choose from.

An unusual shop to stop at while you're in Havre de Grace is the Top of the Bay at 456 Franklin Street. Chat a while with owner Nelson Mengel, who works during the week at American Cyanamid, then comes to his shop on weekends to sell old decoys and baseball cards. He can tell you a lot about the history of the town, and he's not shy in saying who he thinks among the town's promoters loves history and who's just after money. Mengel will tell you that people in Havre de Grace, eager to escape the image of river rats, didn't hesitate to destroy some of the nice old homes by the river and replace them with a parking lot. (Remember the song about paving over paradise?)

At the end of Franklin Street is the Tidewater Grille, where you can sit on the deck and look out at the river, bridges, and boats, and have lunch or a cool drink. There's a good view from inside, too. This place, naturally, specializes in seafood. We had mussels in garlic butter and a cold tuna platter, both of which were quite good. After you eat, you can walk down to the river, where you'll see a couple of small docks, a pontoon named "Dauntless," and a few ducks. You can dock your boat there if you're a customer.

There are other restaurants in Havre de Grace, but they have names like Chat 'n Chew or The Crazy Swede. The Vandiver Inn, a French restaurant with Washington prices, is a bed and breakfast that offers crab cakes, pan-roasted salmon, or filet mignon, and innkeeper Mary McKee is a graduate of the Culinary Institute of America—so the food is probably worth the prices should you wish to indulge. The three-story mansion is listed on the National Historic Register and has eight rooms; call (410) 939-5200.

A block away is the Spencer-Silver Mansion, which dates from 1896 and has been lovingly restored by Carol and Jim Nemeth. It has a large front porch and a huge garden that surrounds the house and is tended by both Carol and Jim. This is a huge old stone house with much of the original stained glass still in place. There are four large rooms, some with big bay windows or a fireplace. Carol's enthusiasm for the details of renovation is contagious; you'll find yourself examining the tile border along the bathroom walls, with large bas relief scallop shells, or the beautifully restored wood fretwork over the doorway upstairs. Call (410) 939-1097.

Havre de Grace may not have the obvious attractions of other shore towns: There's no beach and not much in the way of shopping or entertainment. But it has a quiet charm and a small-town feel that makes it hard to believe you're only 1½ hours from Washington. And if you're like me, the lure of the water never palls, whether it's the river or the bay—or, as in Havre de Grace, both.

NEW MARKET

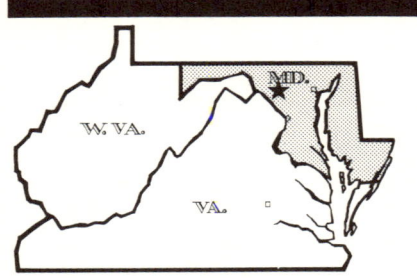

Two kinds of people will enjoy a weekend or a day in New Market, Maryland. The first is the antique buff for whom this is a concentrated opportunity comparable to being let loose in a candy shop. To the second, New Market appeals because it is the small village incarnate, preserved in the 20th century by some miracle that includes both the National Register and enlightened residents. When New Market was laid out in 1793, you could get nightly lodging for 25 cents and a glass of whiskey for 5 cents. Prices have gone up a bit since, but the village (population 850) still looks very much the same as it did two centuries ago.

In the early 1800s, Main Street was the National Road, also known as the Baltimore Turnpike. There were towns like New Market every 8 miles or so—a day's journey when herding farm animals. The street was clogged with Conestoga wagons and farmers driving turkeys to market in Baltimore. When the town was bypassed by the railroad, it passed into obscurity until the first antique shop opened in 1936. Today, New Market bills itself as the antique capital of Maryland. More than 30 shops line the main street; most are open weekends only.

But, shops or no shops, this village is a small, hidden-away anachronism, one of the peaceful relics of the past tucked away in the rolling countryside of Frederick County. If you did nothing else but drop down into the life of the town for a couple of days, you'd enjoy yourself and lower your blood pressure.

Although New Market is only one and a quarter hours from Washington, it's a lovely place to stay overnight. You couldn't do better than the Strawberry Inn at 17 Main Street, run for more than 20 years by Ed and Jane Rossig. These transplanted New Jerseyites used to come to New Market to eat at Mealey's, and noticed a large old dilapidated 1830s farmhouse for sale across the street. It was very run down—"no one wanted it but my husband," says Mrs. Rossig. He fixed it up while she left gratefully for work every day, and they eventually made the house into an inn.

Today, after much hard work by the Rossigs, you would never guess the farmhouse had been in bad shape. You can eat breakfast on the grapevine-covered back porch and take your tea in the gazebo in the back yard. The inn's name comes from

Strawberry Alley on one side, covered with wild strawberries in the summer.

New Market itself is largely a single street—Main Street, of course—with the shops crowding close to the curb, interspersed with benches for resting between shops. You'll find pleasant little gardens and alleys off to the side as you stroll down the street. Nice old trees push the brick sidewalks into humps with roots that have outlasted generations.

You can ease into your weekend slowly: Friday night is quiet, and many shops don't open until 11 or 12 on Saturday morning. By local ordinance, each owner or a tenant must live above the shop. In some of them, you can peer partway up a staircase and dream of a European-style existence, coming downstairs to open your business on Saturday morning.

Another town regulation is that, with a few exceptions, only antique stores are allowed—no tacky souvenir and t-shirt shops. The whole town is a historic district.

The New Market General Store, No. 26, has antique toys and penny candy (remember rows of colored sugar dots on paper?). You can sit down in the back and eat sandwiches or just buy some fudge or a licorice stick and sit by the rain barrels out front and watch the passing parade.

C.W. Wood's Book Shop, No. 42, greets you with the wonderful musty smell of old books when you walk in. Thomas Antiques, No. 60, has refinished, turn-of-the-century, golden oak furniture. For antique jewelry and Japanese netsuke, stop at the Victorian Manor, No. 33.

When you need restoking, go the Village Tea Room, No. 81. It is famous for homemade pies, and it's a cozy place to stop for tea and regrouping.

For more substantial fare, the place to eat is Mealey's, No. 8. Built in 1793, Mealey's started as a store, then was a hotel called the Utz. The construction superintendents who paved the National Pike to accommodate cars, stayed there. Today, an old wooden water pump sits in the main dining room, a reminder of the days when it stood in the back courtyard to serve fresh water to the guests and their horses.

People come from Washington and Baltimore to eat at Mealey's, where the food (the specialties are meat and seafood) is delicious. A special prix fixe on Sunday afternoon is quite popular, judging by the crowds. It's a bustling place, with wooden beams, waitresses singing happy birthday, and a large fireplace in the back by the water pump.

When you have had enough of village life and want to see a little of the countryside, drive 8 miles northeast to Linganore

Winecellars and Berrywine Plantations, where Lucille Aellen will be happy to show you around. We got there five minutes before closing, and she opened everything up and let us taste the extensive wine list for more than an hour. Although Linganore specializes in fruit wines, don't be put off by memories of Boone's Farm. These dry fruit wines bear no relation. With each one, Mrs. Aellen suggested a recipe or a way to drink it (a glass of chilled peach wine before bedtime) that transported us to a sunny summer day.

Mrs. Aellen runs the winery along with her husband Jack, a retired chemist, and son Anthony, the winemaker. They take full advantage of their beautiful setting in the hills of Mount Airy, staging seasonal weekend festivals all year round. Linganore is open every day except major holidays.

If you want to see more of Whittier's "green walled hills of Maryland," you could drive to Emmitsburg to take a look at the shrine of America's first woman saint, Elizabeth Ann Seton, who arrived in the valley in 1809 by covered wagon from Baltimore. A replica of the nation's first parochial school is here, its walls hung with the original samplers made by the first students and the sisters. The shrine has a brief slide show to set things in perspective, and the staff then points the way to the nearby Grotto of Lourdes, where Mother Seton sought peace and spiritual serenity. In spring this grotto in its rural setting can be very beautiful, with its moss-covered rocks, azaleas, and mountain laurel plantings.

FREDERICK COUNTY

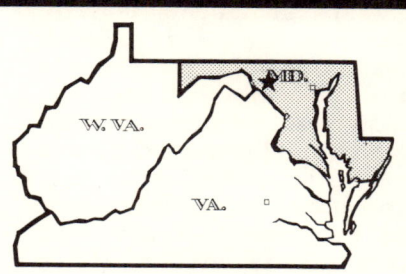

When George Washington came to tea with Barbara Fritchie in Frederick, Maryland, she poured him a cup steaming hot from her very best teapot. That was a couple of hundred years ago and the townspeople are still trying to guess which one it was. The old lady who shook the Union flag in front of Confederate troops marching by her house remains a leading citizen of the town and a lively topic of conversation.

The clustered spires of Frederick stand today much as they did when the National Pike first ran through the heart of the town, and poet John Greenleaf Whittier's green-walled town is still surrounded by the lush farm country of Frederick County. The home of Barbara Fritchie, heroine of a Whittier poem, and that of her parents sit side-by-side as they always did on Patrick Street, and inside is a wonderful window into the life of the town in her time and into the life of the lady herself. The gray dress she wore when she shook the flag from the window hangs in a case. You can see the bed on which she died, and the grand old steel engravings of the Civil War generals and battles that this fierce partisan of the union hung on her walls.

The house is a replica, since her own 1868 home was swept away in a flood by the river which runs close to her back garden. But it's exactly as it once was, with her needlework displayed on the walls and the furniture that was saved back where it always was. The video in the parlor of her parents' home next door is a clever blend of fact and legend and tells us things Whittier never did. We knew she was only 5 feet tall and fierce as a mother eagle, but none of the history books relates that at age 40 she married a 26-year-old glovemaker with whom she lived happily.

Frederick is steeped in yesteryear and is a nice place to visit when you feel like fleeing the 20th century. Stop at the visitors center at 19 East Church Street and let them either guide you or give you a map. You can walk among the families out with their children, the perfume of wisteria heavy in the air, undisturbed by any noise except the birds and the sound of children playing in nearby Baker Park.

Artifacts from the past are everywhere. The bricks in the sidewalk were originally used as ballast in sailing ships. At Trail Mansion at 106 East Church Street, the steppingstone at the curb in front of the wrought iron gate was once used by Frederick gentlewomen getting in and out of their carriages. During the Civil War, prisoners were incarcerated at St. John the Evangelist Catholic Church, and when the organ was moved recently, a prisoner's diary was found written on the wall.

Frederick is good at incorporating history into contemporary life, like the slave quarters at 106 West 2nd Street that now house an art gallery and studio. Every building seems to have steeples, even the fire house and gas station. One of my favorite juxtapositions of old and new is *The Angels in the Architecture* series of *trompe l'oeil* murals painted on various buildings in the historic district by a local artist: A man looks out of a window where a window could easily be, but of course it's really an unbroken wall.

Mount Olivet Cemetery has the graves of Francis Scott Key and Barbara Fritchie, and the American flag flies here night and day, as it does nowhere else, in honor of the father of our national anthem. For kids there is the touch-and-see museum, Rose Hill Manor at 1611 North Market Street, where they can, among other things, play checkers sitting on cracker barrels and using pieces of corncob for counters, or work their initials into a piece of needlework with a threaded needle.

The Tyler-Spite House at 112 West Church Street was built by Dr. John Tyler in 1814 as a way to spite city officials who planned to extend Record Street through there; it is now a bed and breakfast. Frederick is only an hour from Washington, but why not make a weekend of it and explore the town at your leisure; eat dinner at the Brown Pelican on East Church Street; and stop in at the Candy Kitchen on Market Street, which has been selling homemade chocolates since 1902.

Keep going a couple miles farther down Route 85 and you will see signs for Lilypons, where in handsome water gardens every possible water-loving plant, it seems, is grown for sale. All summer the ponds are a riot of color, with white and light pink lotuses riding regally in the pools and water lilies ranging from white to red making shadows for the goldfish who live in the water. Goldfish from here are shipped everywhere and, in this happy environment, grow sometimes to 2 feet. Osprey, egrets, and gulls make meals of the smaller ones; bird watching is part of the fun at Lilypons.

Lilypons's mail order business also offers bullfrogs, which jump from the grassy banks into the pool with a loud "auwark" at the approach of footsteps. Plenty of small water and garden snakes live here too, but there's not much call for them.

For elegant country dining on beautifully kept grounds,

complete with its own goldfish-stocked pool, stop at the Turning Point Inn, a large old Edwardian estate home in Urbana, a few miles south of Frederick on Route 355, (301) 874-2421. It serves dinner with a French accent every night except Monday for a fixed price of $25. Five rooms are available for those who don't feel up to returning to real life after dinner. Or try the Comus Inn, 12 miles from Frederick on Route 109, (301) 428-8593. It's a pleasant 1860 inn at the base of Sugarloaf Mountain, where you can get country food, homemade soups, and relishes. Both have glassed-in porches; reservations are recommended at both.

CARROLL COUNTY

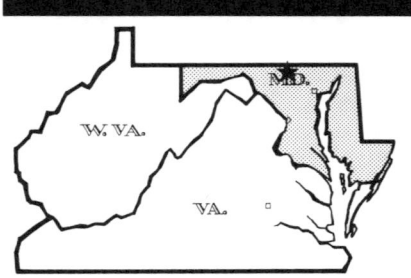

Imagine, if you can, a house that has never changed hands since George Washington was president. Put it down in rural Maryland, only a few miles from an 1813 village officially designated an Historic Area. Add a shopping spree at an international craft shop and some of the most beautiful hilly countryside in the Mid-Atlantic, and you have four good reasons to visit Carroll County.

Carroll County is farm country, and has been ever since the first Germans came here to settle. This is where the harvester and the reaping machine were invented and rural free post delivery was inaugurated. Although Carroll County is becoming more of a Baltimore suburb, it still seems hardly touched by the bustle of urban life—you can tell by the leisurely way the residents react to green traffic lights.

Union Mills Homestead, on Route 97 seven miles north of Westminster, is an old, weathered, gray house that has sheltered six generations of the Shriver family (related to Sargent Shriver, who grew up in Westminster). Nothing in this house has ever been thrown away, from the top hats on the coat rack, inscribed with the name of the wearer and the occasion, to the valentines that came in the mail. This is American history compressed into family archives. It's one of the few historic homes you can tour where nearly everything in the house belonged to the family.

And the Shrivers were quite a family. Two brothers, Andrew and David, built the house and grist mill in 1797. They added a saw mill, a tannery, a blacksmith and cooper shop, and these services brought farmers from the entire countryside. Waiting for their grain to be ground, they stopped a while on the veranda, talking crops and politics. In the days when most area citizens were German-speaking, politicians like Chief Justice Roger Brooke Taney and Francis Scott Key gave speeches from the second floor balcony, and the Shrivers translated them into German for the assembled crowd. Washington Irving sat before the fire here and talked late into the night. James Audubon watched a Baltimore oriole build a nest in one of the willow trees in the back.

In June 1863, Confederate troops camped out back one

night, and Union troops stayed there the next, en route to Gettysburg. The Shriver family resident at that time, Andrew Kaiser, being pro-Union, gave the Union troops a dance in the Homestead's ballroom during their stay.

The house is packed with the domestic possessions of two centuries. On the parlor tables are copies of 1894 *Life* magazines. A scratchy old recording of *Dixie* (an odd choice for Union sympathizers) still plays on the 1911 wind-up Victrola. On the wall is a letter from Thomas Jefferson to David Shriver; the two surveyed the Chesapeake and Delaware Canal together. Also displayed is a certificate stating that the Shrivers donated $1.00 to help build the Washington Monument. In the children's room a dress pattern, complicated as a road map, is spread beside the old sewing machine, and outside the house is a privy ("a three-seater," our guide told us) that has been admired by architects.

Since the Shrivers saved everything, we not only have all the objects, but also all the receipts, so we know how much everything cost: in 1991, they paid $12 a year for phone service for the wall unit they bought that year, and $6 for a baby carriage.

The Homestead is open until 5 P.M., but the last tour of the house or grist mill is at 4 P.M., so allow plenty of time. The surrounding 14-acre park, open until dusk, is a pleasant place to sit and cool off, complete with picnic tables and the sound of water slapping against the wheel of the grist mill.

All Carroll County is picture-pretty, but the lovely little village of Uniontown, just a few miles southwest of Union Mills, is a jewel. The town was made a Registered National Historic District in 1970, so progress can no longer threaten it. Uniontown was settled in 1802, and it must have looked much the same as it does now. The village is one street lined by large maples and handsome old houses. There's not much else but a tiny post office, a single antique store, an 1830 Methodist church, and an elementary school that dates from 1833. Every house has a 19th century date, and most have a wreath on the front door and lace curtains. The homes are surrounded by well-tended gardens with enormous snowball hydrangea bushes and lush herb gardens. On a Sunday afternoon, people rock on their front porches, work in their gardens, or play volleyball, and you think: This is life as it should be lived.

If you would like to prolong your visit to an earlier century, you can stay at Uniontown's bed and breakfast, the Newel Post, (410) 775-2655. The rooms are in a large, rambling 1904 house with stained-glass dormer windows and a big wraparound porch.

Carroll County may be a sleepy spot, but it has an intriguing link with the world of international trade. The International

Gift Shop in New Windsor is a museum-quality outlet for foreign-made handicrafts: baskets from Thailand, Indian brass and batik, woven rugs from Ecuador, wooden bowls from Haiti, and a wide selection of jewelry, all made by artisans trying to escape poverty. The shop is nonprofit; proceeds go direct to the maker.

At the Carroll County Farm Museum, you can make the acquaintance of a turkey, in live form for a change. The turkey is just one of the inmates of this handsome old country place a short distance from downtown Westminster. The museum's central building is the almshouse, which housed Carroll County's poor, insane, hobos, and tramps until 1965, but is now furnished for a wedding in the family of a middle-class farmer of the 19th century. Any curiosity you have about the building's life as a poorhouse will have to be allayed by the printed handout, for the costumed young guide focuses on the more moneyed classes. When the building was taken over by the museum in the 1960s, it was very plain and dirty, but now it has elaborate decorative stencils on the wall and upholstered Victorian chairs. The farmer's study has a "poor man's rug," a floor that has been painted and stenciled, for those who could not afford a more elaborate covering.

After touring the almshouse/farmhouse, you can go into the quilters' room in the crafts building, where you may see three women working on a double wedding ring quilt. When we saw them in June, they had been stitching it for a month and were preparing it for the 4-H fair in August.

Across the way are sheds full of farm equipment. From the 1870 huckster's wagon that used to haul local butter, eggs, and poultry from Uniontown to Baltimore, to the Taylor steam engine, you can get a lightning history of transportation. There's also a pretty flower and herb garden planted with roses and lavender; you can sit on one of the iron benches and soak in the peace. The museum is surrounded by 140 acres with a lake, picnic tables, old shade trees, nature trails, and plenty of space for the kids to run around.

For a stick-to-your-ribs country meal at a bargain price, there's only one place—Baugher's (don't make the mistake I did of pronouncing it Bower's; it's Baucker's). "It's a country place," the woman at the tourist center said, looking at us doubtfully. And it is: most dishes are fried, there's no liquor license, and the decor is simple. But the food is homemade, the service is friendly, the vegetables come from the farm out back, and you get free refills on the homemade cider. Baugher's is where everyone goes after church on Sunday, but it's always crowded—sometimes just for ice cream, which is homemade and 70 cents a scoop. I had a country sausage platter for $5.10: two huge slabs of sausage, apple fritters, banana nut salad, green salad, and apple cider. Of course, if you're used to nouvelle cuisine, you may feel like a nap afterward.

Baugher's has a large selection of produce and plants for sale next door, plus home-baked pies and cookies. A pick-your-own farm offers strawberries, peas, beans, cherries, and black raspberries. Call (410) 848-5541 for a schedule.

Two other farmer's markets are open in the summer. On Saturdays, you can go to the Agriculture Center on Smith Avenue in Westminster or to the Pennsylvania Dutch market at Routes 140 and 97, which is open Fridays as well.

Carroll County, full of beautiful rolling hills, is a dream come true for bicyclists who like to use all their gears, and you can pick up a packet of 10 mapped tours at the Tourism Center at 210 East Main Street. Whether bicycling or driving, you'll pass endless fields of corn and wild clover growing in purple profusion along the side of the road. It's hard to believe you're in the same state that has the flatlands of the Eastern Shore.

If one want a restaurant that is less country, go to Baldwin's at 7618 Main Street in Sykesville, (410) 795-1041. It's housed in the restored Sykesville Depot of the B&O Railroad, which opened in 1884. The decor is Victorian, and some of the dishes are taken from old dining car menus.

Union Mills Homestead, 7 miles north of Westminster on Route 97, is open every day from June 1 to September 1 and weekends in May, September, and October; call (410) 848-2288 for more information. The Carroll County Farm Museum, 500 South Center Street, Westminster, is open from early May to the end of October on weekends and every day except Monday during July and August; call (410) 848-7775 or (410) 876-2667. The International Gift Shop, New Windsor Service Center, on Route 31 seven miles southwest of Westminster, is open from 9 A.M. to 5 P.M. Monday through Saturday (closed on Sunday except in December); call (410) 635-8711.

GARRETT COUNTY

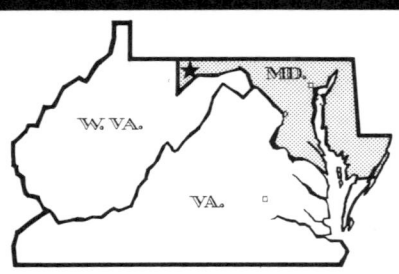

Because the prediction was for rain all weekend, I thought it would be a bad time to visit Garrett County, a place whose attractions were mainly outdoors. I couldn't have been more wrong. It did rain all day Saturday of that last weekend in October, but we found several hospitable indoor places with roaring fires and people happy to talk to us while we warmed ourselves. The next day, Halloween (perhaps appropriately), we woke to snow—and I discovered what a different experience snow is in the country than in the city (especially Washington), when you have to get in your car and drive to work with a lot of nervous drivers. It was a wonderful place to see the first snow of the season. Our hostess at the Casselman Valley Farm, who had seen 4 feet of snow on her property the year before, thought nothing of a little October snowfall.

Garrett County is one of Maryland's little-known treasures. While Deep Creek Lake has its fans both summer and winter, it doesn't seem to have been discovered the way the Chesapeake Bay has. In the 3-hour drive from Washington, you will feel as if you are in another world—and as far as weather patterns, you are. The county gets as average 82 inches of snow a year, more than parts of Alaska.

The fun starts on the drive there. On mountain roads, you pass through towns with names like Piney Grove and Flintstone and are treated to breathtaking vistas at every turn—especially if you're lucky enough to go in the fall. Eventually you will get to Grantsville, a village of 500 hardy souls just off Interstate 68 on Alternate Route 40, the old National Pike.

Grantsville is the oldest settlement and one of only eight incorporated towns in Garrett County. It has a few places to eat and to stay overnight and a place where you can buy local handicrafts, but don't look for souvenir shops or antique emporiums. Garrett County is very low key; that's part of its charm. But I met some of the friendliest people there I've seen while doing this book—and you don't get the feeling it's just because they make their living from tourists.

In the mid-18th century, Grantsville was a stop for stagecoaches traveling west on the National Pike—at one point, 14 a day passed by each way. Turkeys, pigs, and sheep roamed freely;

pigs lay down in the road when they felt like it; and turkeys wandered off into the trees.

Traveling farmers and drovers stayed at the Little Crossings Inn, built in 1818 and now the only log tavern left on the National Pike. Today, it is the Penn Alps crafts shop and restaurant, a large old wooden beam building with several dining rooms and large stone fireplaces. Enjoy the delicious smell of fresh baked bread and chocolate cake for sale at the entrance, then ask to see the Dunbar Room in the back. You can't eat there unless you have a large party, but its two-story, double-stone fireplace is worth a look.

Across from Penn Alps is the Spruce Forest Artisan Village, one of the nicest manmade attractions in Garrett County. This collection of six log cabins, restored and moved here from elsewhere in western Maryland or just over the border in Pennsylvania, houses working artisans from Memorial Day weekend until the last Saturday in October. These are not just people practicing their hobbies for the benefit of tourists; they are serious, skilled artists. Gary Yoder, a Garrett County native, has been carving and painting birds for more than 20 years and has several works displayed in museums. A reserved man who clearly loves birds, Yoder says, "This validates my bird watching." Ann Jones, a Pittsburgh transplant, fell in love with the countryside and moved to the area. She is a fourth grade schoolteacher and a weaver, surrounded in her log studio by vibrantly colored rugs, scarves, shawls, and tunics (the artists sell their wares in their studios).

The artisan village is the brainchild of Dr. Alta Schrock, a delightful woman who is usually somewhere on the premises (she lives in a cabin on the property). Dr. Schrock, who doesn't mind telling you she's 82, got a Ph.D. in biology back when some universities told her outright they would not admit her to their program because she was a woman. But she persevered and went on to teach college for more than 40 years, until she turned her attention to moving the log cabins here and finding artists to use them as studios. "History's an avocation," says Dr. Schrock, and she feels strongly that not only the buildings but also the crafts should be preserved.

She must, because moving a log cabin several miles sounds like quite a project. One of the cabins was built in 1835 by Benedict Miller, the first Amish bishop in the area and Dr. Schrock's great-great-great-grandfather. Succeeding generations used the building as a farmhouse and a butcher shop, so it was pretty messy by the time Dr. Schrock decided to have it moved and restored in the 1980s. It was brought floor by floor from a few miles away in Springs, Pennsylvania, on a flatbed truck. Today, it is set up like a home, sparsely furnished, as befits its original Amish inhabitant. Upstairs is a foot locker belonging to Dr. Schrock's distant cousin Alvin Miller, a Mennonite relief worker who traveled from Grantsville to feed the hungry in Russia in the 1920s.

Every year on the second full weekend in July, the artisan village has a summerfest and quilt show displaying the products of some 70 craftspeople and quilters from Maryland, Pennsylvania, West Virginia, and elsewhere. The festival is Thursday, Friday, and Saturday; like much else in this church-oriented county, the artisan village is closed on Sunday. Penn Alps restaurant used to be closed Sunday, until a non-Mennonite manager was hired just for that day.

When you're done at Penn Alps, walk over the Casselman stone bridge. It was built in 1818 to ease the flow of riverboat traffic on the C&O Canal, but in the end, the canal was not extended beyond Cumberland. When it was built, the bridge was the largest single span stone arch bridge in the country, at 80 feet. To make sure the bridge wouldn't collapse (as widely predicted) at the public ceremony where the supporting timbers were to be removed, the contractor loosened them the night before. The next day, he stood under the bridge during the ceremony to show his confidence in its stability.

Most visitors to Garrett County are attracted by Deep Creek Lake, a manmade lake covering almost 4,000 acres. Many people come there to boat or fish in the summer. There's a sandy beach with a lifeguard in Deep Creek Lake State Park, and even a water slide nearby. The lake has a different kind of attraction in the winter; in the middle of the season, it is covered by 18 inches of ice. Maryland's only ski resort, Wisp, is next door in McHenry.

Garrett County has a great number of state parks, where, depending on the season, you can go whitewater rafting (on the appropriately named Savage River), hunting, snowmobiling, or just hiking and picnicking. There are so many parks and forests that it's hard to imagine them ever feeling crowded.

A friend who heard I was going to Garrett County said doubtfully, "Let me know if you find any good place to eat." And I did: a cozy, wood and stone restaurant overlooking Deep Creek Lake called the Silver Tree Inn. It has several reasonably priced Italian dishes every night, plus nightly specials like prime rib and salmon en papillote. If the huge TV screen on one wall is off-putting, ask for seating in a different part of the large dining room. At last check, the Silver Tree doesn't take reservations, but the number is (301) 334-2308. The Deer Park Inn in Oakland, listed on the National Register of Historic Places, is also reputed to be good; its chef comes from Washington's Ritz Carlton and Jockey Club. Reservations recommended: (301) 334-2308.

Your choice of overnight accommodation in Garrett County ranges from a wilderness campsite to the Alpine Village, a group of efficiencies on Deep Creek Lake, complete with their own fireplaces. But for my money (and not much of it), you can't beat the Casselman Valley Farm, a bed and breakfast in a 100-year-old farmhouse. When we called from Penn Alps to check our directions, our hostess said, "I'll just send my daughter-in-law to meet you." We insisted this wasn't necessary, and indeed her directions were fine—just be sure and turn left at the Casselman Lumber Company. When we met, she said, "You can call me Sis, or Mary."

Sis had left a note on the door in case we got there early (no one locks doors in Garrett County, apparently) because she had been at a lumber company auction, stocking up on plywood and wooden doors. As she led us up to our room, she pointed out the breakfast nook, which she had not only built but filled with creatures of the season (it was October 30): a table of four life-size goblins and witches, with black capes, rubber masks, and yarn hair, feasting on large plastic spiders and straw.

Sis is clearly a collector. Downstairs is a juke box like the kind on "Happy Days." Our room, the Princess Room, had an enormous blue stuffed bear on the floor, little kewpie dolls on the bureau, and a lovely view of the farm and the countryside.

When we came back from dinner, we stopped in the living room to respond to the greeting of a woman on the sofa whom I assumed was Sis's daughter or daughter-in-law. It turned out she was a guest, there for the weekend with her husband, who had come so many times that she and Sis were now fast friends. We all stood in the kitchen and talked about country life, old houses, snow, and whatever else came to mind.

The next afternoon we started back home after driving around in the snow all morning—20 miles from Casselman Valley there was not a flake in sight, and we wondered if we had dreamed it all.

The number for the Casselman Valley Farm is (301) 895-3419. The Deep Creek Lake-Garrett County Promotion Council, (301) 334-1948, can tell you about other places to stay and anything else you want to know.

THE TRAIL OF JOHN WILKES BOOTH

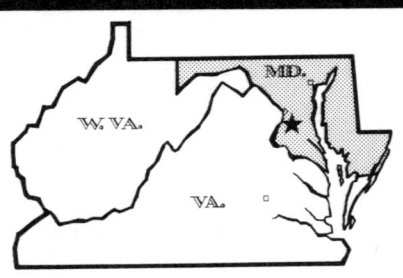

The small bay horse was nervous, but the rider looked completely at ease. He answered the sergeant's questions without hesitation and looked every inch the gentleman. He said he did not know about the curfew; he had been waiting for the moon to rise. His name was Booth, and he lived in Charles County near Beantown. The sergeant posted at the bridge across the river allowed him to pass. He was to say later that the gentleman seemed "a proper person." Not surprising. John Wilkes Booth was an actor, and nothing of the pain in his broken left leg—or whatever emotions he felt after having shot the president of the United States a short time before—showed in his handsome face.

He was bound for Surratt Tavern in Surrattsville (now Clinton), Prince Georges County, where he had planned to pick up binoculars and carbines for himself and his conspirator, David Herold, and now, because of the pain, also a good jolt of whiskey. The two of them, meeting along the road, made it there by midnight, after a 10-mile ride through what was then known as Washington County. It took them just a bit more than an hour and a half from the time Booth shot President Lincoln in his box at Ford's Theatre.

More than 120 years later, this seems incredible. The curious traveler who today tries to follow Booth's trail quickly discovers the hard reality. The road he took on the night of April 14, 1865, through the streets of Washington is no longer muddy, but it is tortuous. It leads through the back roads of Anacostia, through a thousand red traffic lights, under and over and through a spaghetti of tunnels and overpasses and turnings, where you lose your way in spite of the most careful directions.

Why go this way when you could take Maryland Route 5 and be there in short order? We wanted to imagine what Booth must have been thinking, galloping past the Capitol whose power he so hated, feeling the pain of his shattered fibula bone poking through the flesh of his leg, worrying whether he would make the planned rendezvous with Herold, knowing that, in a moment at Ford's Theatre, he had thrown away a promising career and had become a hunted man.

Once at the Surratt House (the tavern) in Clinton, Maryland, it's easy to step back into the 19th century and imagine Booth's arrival. The Civil War and that April night in 1865 are hardly dusty history here in southern Maryland, where the past is a matter of grave importance. Although the town's name was changed from Surrattsville in the 1860s, when John Surratt lost the postmastership, some residents still call it that. Not everybody you talk to will admit it, but the Confederate cause is still alive and well in southern Prince George's and Charles counties. Only one man in Prince George's voted for Lincoln in 1860 and this is not forgotten.

Family connections are kept alive through the years here. Davey Herold, the 20-year-old drugstore clerk who rode with Booth that night, is a distant cousin of Laurie Verge, manager and historian of the Surratt House. He spent the night before the assassination of Lincoln in Ms. Verge's great-grandfather's house in T.B. (a small community on Route 5 at the junction of Routes 373 and 381), leaving behind a nightshirt with John Surratt's name on it, probably picked up by mistake in a meeting of the conspirators.

Under the docent's guidance, the tavern comes alive. In 1865, it was run by Bill Lloyd, a D.C. policeman who was his own best customer at the bar. It was also a post office, so the men could have a drink when they came in to get their mail. Ladies, of course, were not allowed to enter the tavern.

You can see where the 19th century wayfarer sat with a friend over a game of checkers; at this table they sat with a tot to take out the cold and had tobacco-spitting contests. In this room the traveler could eat a robust meal for 50 cents; upstairs he might spend the night for 25 cents and share the bed with other travelers. The arms for the conspiracy were stashed behind the wainscoting in the loft above the dining room; the first plan was to kidnap the president, and arms would be needed. In the parlor of the family quarters, in which the Surratts lived with their three children, is Mary Surratt's exquisite little desk, and in the hall hangs her portrait painted from the only known photograph, taken at 28 or 30. Her stern expression reminds modern viewers that then you had you had your photograph taken rarely; it was a formal occasion, and it was unlikely you would smile.

Mrs. Surratt (as she is respectfully called in this house) was a proper Catholic lady married to a Confederate sympathizer. Her role in the murder is debated to this day. The court found her guilty, and she was hanged for her part in the plot—the first woman to be executed by the U.S. government.

By the time Booth arrived that night in 1865, John Surratt

had been dead for a few years. He was rather a feckless man—he never even had the money to paint the house, which had only the primer coat. He died leaving his widow in debt, but he did leave her a rooming house on H Street in Washington (it's a Chinese restaurant now). Our tour guide debates: We do know that Mrs. Surratt knew Booth and that the conspirators plotted the assassination in her rooming house—but women were rarely privy to politics then. At the trial, everyone said, "How could this gentle Christian woman be involved in a murder plot?"

Lloyd was no less Confederate-minded than John Surratt had been, and the Surratt tavern was known as a safe house in the active underground for southern spies. It was well situated for this, perched on the little hill near the road—New Cut they called it in those days, the main north-south road in 1865. Today it's called Old Brandywine; it's paved, but still a country road. When the carbine rifles were brought to the Surratt tavern for future use, Lloyd objected because the houses there were constantly being searched because of their proximity to Washington.

Booth never even dismounted at the Surratt tavern that fateful night. Instead, he sent Herold to pound on the door to wake Lloyd, who was drunk but stumbled down with the binoculars, the carbines, and a bottle of whiskey from which both men took a long draught.

And what sort of young man was Herold? Was his rage against the Union equal to Booth's? Why did he do it?

"Davey's problem was that he had seven sisters," says Ms. Verge. "Booth's attraction for Davey was male companionship."

In an exhibit in a building next to the Surratt House is a case with letters from the Surratt daughters to their friends. "Father has been entertaining a gentleman from across the Potomac," writes Anna in one. "Spies," explains Verge.

When Booth and Herold left the Surratt tavern they were looking for a doctor for Booth's broken left leg and the name of Dr. Samuel Mudd came to mind. Dr. Mudd was known to be a Confederate sympathizer and Booth had met him in Washington. The doctor, whose farmhouse was 30 miles south of Washington, would surely help them, they figured, so they turned their horses south. The house, on Route 382, is open to the public and the doctor's descendants show you around.

It was 4 A.M. when Herold pounded on the Mudd door asking for help for Booth, who by this time had applied a stage beard. The doctor got out of bed and let them in. They gave their names as Tyson and Tyler and said that the horse had fallen on Booth's leg. You can see the room Booth was brought to, where Dr. Mudd cut off his boot and made him a splint from a hatbox.

Herold joined the Mudd family for dinner the next day and asked about a carriage or other conveyance for the wounded man. They couldn't get one, so they decided to leave on horseback. As the men went downstairs, Mrs. Mudd saw Booth's beard move, and her suspicions were aroused. She said to Herold, "You should stay here until your friend is better," to which he reportedly replied, "No, I'll take him to my lady love."

Mrs. Mudd mentioned their guest's disguise to her husband. By this time, Dr. Mudd had heard in town about the assassination of the president, and he wanted to report the two men to the authorities. Mrs. Mudd refused to let her husband leave her and their four small children with the two strangers, so they reported the men when they went to church the next day. When a servant girl was cleaning out the room where Booth had stayed, she found a boot with "J.W. Booth" written on it, which Mrs. Mudd gave to the authorities. "It was used as evidence against him," our tour guide says bitterly.

When the Union soldiers on Booth's trail got word of his stop at the Mudd house, they came there and tore the place apart, burning the fences and destroying the crops. Mrs. Mudd and her children were held hostage in the bedroom. "She was helpless," says our guide. "The soldiers didn't care whether she and the children had anything to eat." Worse, "The government never restituted the Mudd family for one cent."

When Dr. Mudd was tried, a military tribunal voted for life imprisonment by one vote—one more vote, and he would have been hanged with Mary Surratt and the others. He served his time at Fort Jefferson, Florida, near Key West. When a yellow fever epidemic broke out, Dr. Mudd took care of the prisoners, because the prison doctor was among the first to be stricken. The prisoners and guards were so grateful they sent a petition to President Andrew Johnson asking that Dr. Mudd be freed for his help fighting yellow fever. The president was busy with his own impeachment trial, but he did manage to pardon Mudd a week before he left office.

You won't get the impression Dr. Mudd recognized Booth from his granddaughter, Louise Mudd Arehart. Wearing an 1860s skirt and standing behind the counter of the gift shop in the rear of the Mudd home, Mrs. Arehart is the final arbitrator in matters around the house. She is a woman of decided opinions, and the chief one is that her grandfather has gotten a bum rap. She has made it her life's work to have Dr. Mudd vindicated and thinks Laurie Verge ought to have done the same for her ancestors.

There's not that much to see in the Mudd house—much of

the furniture is "of the period" rather than original—but the fun is hearing the story from the doctor's descendants, or from docents who have been primed by Mrs. Arehart. Asked how the docents know details like Dr. and Mrs. Mudd's argument over who should answer Herold's late night knock on the door, Mrs. Arehart says, "I teach them. I was brought up with this." She was the last baby born in this house, the youngest of 33 grandchildren (Dr. Mudd had nine children). She wears the wedding and engagement ring given by her father, Samuel Mudd, Jr., to her mother, and shows them off proudly.

Downstairs in the house is a portrait of Mudd done by his great-grandson, Bernie Cox, and the original sideboard, which Dr. Mudd's wife had sent to auction to pay his legal fees—but years later, Mrs. Arehart traced it and got it back. "That's one good thing about there being so many Mudds in the area," says our docent. "If you have to auction off something, it's not hard to keep track of who has it and get it back."

In the living room is a secretary made by Dr. Mudd while he was in prison. When he wasn't tending to yellow fever victims, he did woodwork and sent his creations home to pay his legal fees. Also on display is a photo of Edward, Dr. Mudd's son, a D.C. policeman who was detailed—what else?—to protect the president. In another irony, the dining room has two chairs from Ford's Theatre.

Upstairs is a chest made by Ned Spangler, who held Booth's horse behind Ford's Theatre while the deed was done. He was imprisoned along with Dr. Mudd and also pardoned by the president. They became friends at Fort Jefferson (Spangler nursed the doctor through his yellow fever), and when Spangler was freed, he made his way back to the Mudd house. Unfortunately, he arrived at night and a dog chased him up a tree, where he stayed all night. The next morning, all were reunited, and Spangler lived with the Mudds for the last 6 years of his life.

The real reason Mrs. Arehart worked so hard to get the old Mudd home renovated and turned into a museum comes down to visits by her late grandfather. More than 20 years ago, at her home in La Plata, she heard knocking on the door and footsteps going up and down the stairs—but there was never anyone there. Then she started to see a man in the house, but could never see his face clearly. Eventually, she realized it was Dr. Mudd, and his message was that his old home should be rescued from its state of disrepair. She set to work writing senators and congressmen and organized the Committee for the Restoration of the Samuel A. Mudd House. In 1974, the house was listed on the National Register of Historic Places.

The rest of Booth's escape route can be traced through hiding places in the pines near Rich Hill, the spot at Dent's Meadow near Pope's Creek where the two fugitives set out in a boat for the Virginia shore, and the Garrett farm where they were captured. (For the dedicated history buff, a poster showing the route is available at the Surratt House gift shop.) After making a wreckage of the Surratt tavern and the Mudd home, Union soldiers caught up with Booth and Herold 11 days later, and there was a shootout. To this day we don't know if Booth tried to commit suicide or was shot by a soldier. It's all a long time ago. And still, in school playgrounds here and there, little girls with jump ropes chant at playmates who miss the twirling rope:

> You missed, your name is Mudd.
> You missed, your name is Mudd.

If you'd like to break your journey through history with a stop for lunch, try Gena's Crab House in Clinton. This is a no-frills place with a juke box full of country songs, Bud on tap, and good seafood. Or, continue south after the Mudd House down Route 301 to Pope's Creek, where there are several large seafood restaurants that look out on the water.

The Surratt House is open from March to mid-December; call (301) 868-1121. The Mudd House is open late March through late November; call (301) 645-6870 or (301) 934-8464.

ANNAPOLIS WALKING TOUR

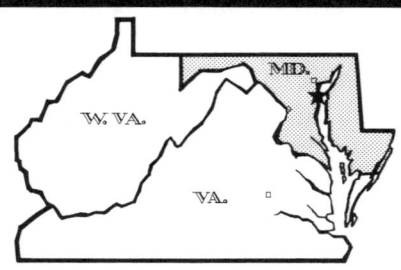

There are several ways to see Annapolis—from a boat on the Severn River or the Chesapeake Bay, from inside one of the many good seafood restaurants, or from a tour of the shops along Main Street. The way I had seen it most often was from Route 50 on the way to the Eastern Shore —until I took the walking tour offered by Three Centuries Tours of Annapolis. It's a pleasant town to walk around on your own, with the harbor view, the brick sidewalks, the hilly walks. But you get a much better flavor led by a guide in 17th century garb who has a fascination with maritime history and is bursting with stories of historical figures that he can't wait to share.

The enthusiasm of our guide was contagious. A courtly gentleman who called us blue-jeaned tourists "sir" and "ma'am," he seemed at home in his red cape and tights, knee breeches, and three-cornered hat. He explained that the more buttons you wore in the 17th century, the richer you were, and his eight did not speak of much wealth.

The afternoon tour starts at Gibson's Lodgings, a historic home converted to a bed and breakfast. It has a red plaque, which means it dates from about 1870. All Annapolis homes from 1694 to 1910 have a colorful plaque, eight colors for eight different periods. Our guide said cheerily that the town hasn't changed much since 1694. Annapolis was named in honor of Princess Anne, later Queen Anne. The man who designed the town, Governor Francis Nicholson, laid out both Annapolis and Williamsburg and was governor of both Virginia and Maryland.

You spend a good part of the tour seeing the Naval Academy, which, our guide reminded us, is really your property since it is supported by U.S. taxpayers. Even if you have no military connections, it's fascinating to learn about this culture, which is truly unlike any other. In Bancroft Hall—the world's largest dorm, housing 4,200 midshipmen and women—you see a typical student room. Textbooks must be arranged in order of size, and the rooms get the white glove treatment for dirt and the black glove treatment in the shower for soap suds. No phones or TVs are allowed in the rooms.

The rest of Bancroft Hall is worth a look. You won't be able to go to the upper floors where the students live (their rooms occupy 25 miles of corridor). Even their parents can visit them in their rooms only one day a year, on Parents' Day. But the rotunda at the entryway is quite impressive, with very high ceilings and a mural of the battleship South Dakota, from World War II, on one side. Upstairs, in Memorial Hall, are the largest crystal chandeliers you will probably ever see and a granite memorial with the names of all the Naval Academy graduates who died in battle. You can look through the window down into the dining hall, where, every day at noon, the students must march into lunch together in formation.

The first-year students, the plebes, are "lower than low," said our guide. The night they arrive, they are given a book of rules, and questions about the contents are fired at them starting at 5:30 the next morning, until 9:30 at night. If they don't know the answers, they are given a certain number of pushups to do—with the result, presumably, that the more ignorant end up being more physically fit. You are not surprised to hear that 20 percent of the class leaves the academy in their first year.

Another quaint Naval Academy tradition: The graduating class tapes and glues a cap on top of Herndon Monument, a 200-foot-high vertical structure on the campus. The monument is then greased with lard, and it is up to the plebes to work together to retrieve the cap, which they do by forming a human pyramid.

Be sure and look at Tecumseh, the bronze bust of a Delaware Indian, known as the god of 2.0, as in grade point average. As you pass him on your way to an exam, you're supposed to toss a penny into his basket, above your head. If it lands, that means you will pass your exam. The middies may give him a salute, but with the left hand. Right-handed salutes are only for military officers.

The Academy chapel is a scheduled stop on the tour, but if there's a wedding there, you might not be able to go inside. The ceremonies are tightly scheduled in May, since the middies are not allowed to marry until after they graduate. There is a small industry of women in Annapolis called pushers who hire themselves out to dress and prepare brides for naval weddings. The time limit is 45 minutes; after that, the brides are pushed out the door into the chapel.

In the chapel, each stained glass window has a biblical quote with a nautical theme—Old Testament on one side, New Testament on the other. At the end is a Tiffany window of Christ walking on the water.

Even if a wedding prevents you from seeing the chapel, you can view the tomb of John Paul Jones underneath. He was who the Navy got when they wanted the first U.S. naval hero, even though he was Scots rather than American. Like a lot of heroes, he was flamboyant and egotistical. When he died in Paris in 1792, he was buried in a lead coffin and preserved so carefully in alcohol that when he was dug up by the U.S. Navy 150 years later, he was a perfect leather corpse. Now, he's in a crypt made of a special mottled marble from the Pyrenees that makes you think of the sea in turmoil. At the perimeter you will find artifacts and quotes from John Paul. My favorite is inscribed in a case under his sword: "I wish to have no concern with any ship that does not sail fast, for I intend to go in harm's way."

Before you leave the Academy campus, you'll stop in the U.S. Naval Academy Museum with its wonderful display of ship models. Some of them are over 150 years old, and there's a whole room of ships made by French prisoners in the late 18th and early 19th centuries from beef or mutton bones saved from their prisoners' rations. They immersed the bones in wet clay to make them more pliable, then added rigging made from human or horse hair. It looks a lot like scrimshaw. You keep thinking, only the French could look at the (no doubt) unappetizing prisoners' meals and think, I could create something beautiful with the leftover bones.

Walking out onto Maryland Avenue, you stop in front of the Chase-Lloyd house. This was built for Samuel Chase, one of the four signers of the Declaration of Independence from Maryland. It's in the Georgian style, brick and very symmetrical, down to fake doors that open onto brick walls but provide needed balance. Francis Scott Key later married a Lloyd in this house. Under the will of a descendant, the home was to be used to house elderly women of modest income (not so modest that they are charity cases) and good reputation. And so it is: Eight women lived there at last count.

Across the street is the Hammond-Harwood House, a somewhat grander five-part building in the Georgian style. It was started in 1774 but was never finished because the supply of materials from England stopped when the Revolutionary War started. After the war, Mr. Hammond, who had been on the wrong side, returned to England. You can pick up a copy of their highly regarded Maryland cookbook on your visit.

The next stop is St. John's College on King George Street, founded as a boys school in the 1600s. Students there used the Horn Book, a small board with a few lessons written on it, made of melted cow horn, paper, and glue. It is shaped like a paddle and apparently was used as one, too. George Washington came to visit the school, and the founders wanted to name it Washington

College. But a school in Chestertown, Maryland, on the Eastern Shore, got the idea first. St. John was chosen instead because he was the patron saint of the Masons, and George Washington was a Mason.

On the campus of the college is the country's only standing liberty tree. They were scattered around the colonies in pre-revolutionary times, and anyone who wanted to talk rebellion against the king did it under these trees. If an official walked by, the rebels simply changed the subject.

In the 1840s, the students at St. John's tried to blow up the tree with gunpowder—it was being eaten away by insects—but they forgot to put the gunpowder in a capsule, so it just burned. With five pounds, there was quite a fire. It had a good result: All the insects were killed, and the tree was saved. Now there's a 15-foot cavity filled with concrete where the gunpowder was. Tree experts say the 600-year-old tulip poplar should live another 600 years.

Whether you go on the Three Centuries Tour or not, you must see the statehouse. It is the oldest continuously used statehouse in the country, in use since 1694. During the seven months in 1784 that Annapolis was the capital of the young United States, this building was the U.S. Capitol. It has a double dome, topped by a carved acorn, an 18th century symbol of wisdom and longevity, from the owl.

Inside, you can see the room where George Washington resigned his commission to the Continental Congress in 1793 and where the Treaty of Paris was signed. Ladies were not allowed to be present when affairs of state were conducted because of their reputation as chatterboxes; they could sit in the balcony only.

Outside this room is a 200-year-old staircase, secured with pegs not nails. It leads to the mezzanine, but the door at the top cannot be opened. This dates from the 1920s, when a dishonest governor used the staircase to sneak into his office while instructing his secretary to say he wasn't in. When the legislature found out, they stopped it by shutting off the door. But since the staircase is 200 years old, no one wants to tear it down.

The governor's mansion, across from the statehouse, was not occupied by Governor Schaefer because he is a bachelor, our guide said, and did not want citizens knowing his comings and goings. The small park in front of the statehouse and the mansion has an area called Lawyer's Walk, where anyone can come and scream complaints against the governor, much like Speaker's Corner in London's Hyde Park.

After walking for two hours, you will be ready for a seafood meal in one of Annapolis's many good restaurants. Try Harbour

House, with a big second floor room with a view of the harbor and outdoor tables for nice days. For a mini-vacation, stay in town overnight, and try the 1772 Maryland Inn, (800) 847-8882. This nice old wedge-shaped inn is the perfect antidote to cookie-cutter motels, a hotel rescued from modernization by Historic Annapolis in 1956. It was built on ground set aside in 1694 for the use of the Town Drummer "in a dry and healthy part of the city." You can eat gourmet food in the inn's 18th century Treaty of Paris Restaurant, or hear Charlie Byrd play jazz guitar at the King of France Tavern.

The number for Three Centuries Tours is (410) 263-5401.

CHESTERTOWN AND THE EASTERN NECK

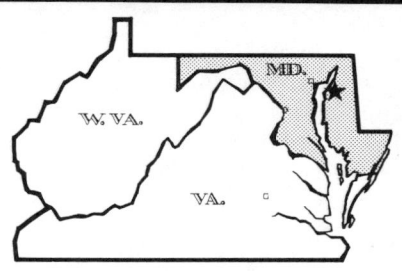

Chestertown's finest hour was some 250 years ago. Then, it was an important Maryland seaport and its leading citizens were busy shaping American freedom, enlisting in its navy, and even holding their own "tea party" in the harbor. Rich merchants built Georgian and Federal homes topped with widow's walks along the waterfront, and ladies of fashion walked Water Street under their parasols.

But Baltimore's harbor soon surpassed Chestertown's and industry followed the ships across the bay. And what could be more fortunate for us 20th century visitors who, because of this, can take a look at a town suspended in its past?

A visit to Chestertown is nice any time, but if you go in late May you'll be on hand for the re-enactment of the 1774 tossing of the tea in the harbor. Costumed actors shove tea baled in burlap into the water from a skipjack in imitation of their Boston compatriots. The matter is debated up and down High Street by angry citizens incensed over English taxes while some counsel caution for fear of retaliation. High Street is blocked off for all this so that no anachronistic cars can bother public orators or the craftsmen who set up shop in 18th century arts. A parade innocent of motor cars winds down High Street on Saturday.

Part of the fun of Chestertown is that it's an escape from crowds into a more leisured era. Pick up a walking tour map at the Town Hall, 118 North Cross Street, or if that's closed, at Scottie's Shoe Store on High Street. Walk down High Street to the Customs House at Water and High Streets, the center of the sugar trade with the British West Indies in the 1730s. It was near this spot that on May 23, 1774, irate citizens boarded the brigantine *Geddes* and threw the tea cargo into the Chester River. Across the street is the Hynson-Ringgold House, the front of which was built by the famous William Buckland in 1771. For the last 50 years, it has been the home of the presidents of Washington College, founded in 1782 with financial help from George Washington.

One of the town's most elaborate houses is Widehall, on Water Street across from the Customs House. This mansion, complete with thick, two-story Ionic columns and a lovely large garden, is right on the water and must have a magnificent view of the river from its second floor. It was built by Thomas Smythe, the head of Maryland's revolutionary Provisional Government from 1774 to 1776.

Widehall is privately owned, so you must walk past it to the public landing at the end of High Street, where you can spend a peaceful few moments sitting on a wooden bench and gazing out at the river. You can see the bridge over which you entered Chestertown on your left, and the marina on your right. (Next to the marina is the Old Wharf Inn, which serves seafood and offers a good view of the river.)

As you walk down Water Street, toward the bridge, peer past the gates of the 18th century homes at the beautiful gardens on the waterfront. Turning onto Maple Avenue will propel you into the next century and large houses with Victorian gables. Many of the houses in Chestertown, even the tiny ones, have front porches with rocking chairs, giving a nice, neighborly feeling. Some of the large old homes have widow's walks facing the river.

At 231 High Street is one reason a lot of people come to Chestertown: the White Swan Tavern, dating back to 1733. Over the years, it has been a tavern, a lumber and hardware business, a shoe store, and news agency—and, since 1981, a bed and breakfast restored to its 1795 appearance. Owner Horace Havemeyer, Jr., is a New Yorker who fell in love with this part of Maryland and has spared no research or expense to turn this old building into a well-appointed overnight stop. Havemeyer even journeyed to Ireland in quest of marble to match the original fireplace in the game room, after an archeological dig at the tavern site turned up a scrap of stone. He had the scrapings of paint chemically analyzed to come up with the truly surprising bright blue in the tavern room.

Afternoon tea is served there, with homemade sweets and tea specially blended for the inn. If you stay in one of the five rooms, you can have your breakfast in one of the antique-furnished parlors or, if the weather's nice, on the back patio. You may find the service a bit lackadaisical here, but there's no question it's a beautiful old inn.

An excellent restaurant with reasonable prices is the Ironstone Cafe at 236 Cannon Street. It is a cheerful place with ironstone china in the windows, and the skylight brings in lots of sun at lunchtime. For truly elegant lodgings and fine dining, go to the Imperial Hotel, 208 High Street. Some rooms have porches overlooking High Street, and the meals are expensive but reputedly very good (awards from the *Wine Spectator* hang on the walls). Brunch is served on the patio. The Cellar at the Imperial, a small basement shop, has unusual crafts and jewelry.

When you have walked and eaten and want to set a spell, find a bench in the little park at Cross and High Streets, near the Town Hall. In the center of the park is a big fountain with layers of lions and craning swans, topped by a goddess cradling a seashell. Have a look at the shops on Cross Street: the Chester River Knitting Company sells sweaters, and the Corsica Bookstore offers a very good selection of books on the Chesapeake Bay.

And don't miss the bronze statue by the Town Hall: Chestertown's native son William "Swish" Nicholson. Legend has it that only he and Babe Ruth have ever been walked intentionally with the bases loaded. Who could resist the solemn inscription: "This statue of a baseball great is placed here as a tribute to the man, as an inspiration to the nation's youth and as a reminder that sport is important to the American dream."

Continue in your car on High Street out of town until it becomes Route 20, then turn left onto Route 446 and right onto Ricauds Branch-Langford Road. You're now on one of the first turnpikes in the country, the route that Tench Tilghman, secretary and aide to General George Washington, took for his famous ride from Virginia to Philadelphia to tell the Continental Congress of Cornwallis's surrender during the Revolutionary War.

On this road you will find St. Paul's Episcopal Church. Services have been held here since the building went up in 1713, and it's well worth a stop. On the church grounds, you'll see boxwood, a huge old spruce, luxuriant crepe myrtle, and a couple of oak trees that are 300 years old. Actress Tallulah Bankhead is buried in the cemetery, as is Michael Miller, "donor of this sacred churchyard," who died in 1699. One of the oldest inscriptions, for Daniel Coley, who died in 1729, has been thoughtfully re-incised so we can read it:

> Behold and see now here I lye
> As you are now so once was I
> As I am now so must you be
> Therefore prepare to follow me.

The early settlers were not known for their lighthearted attitude.

If you go back to Route 20, you can take it to Rock Hall, a small town right on the Chesapeake Bay that has the distinction of being 4 miles from the Bay Bridge by water and 40 miles by land. Head for the Waterman's Crab House on Sharp Street Wharf. It's easy to find—just go to the bottom of the hill and toward the water. The Crab House has a 40-foot deck overlooking the harbor, from which you can see the Bay Bridge, passing sailboats, and osprey. You can have a drink—or better yet, let the waitress cover your table with brown paper and bring you a plate of crabs—and watch the sunset. It doesn't get any better than this on a summer night.

Rock Hall also has what must be the world's smallest public beach, down Beach Road. You can swim there, but there's no lifeguard. There are picnic tables if you prefer just to sit and gaze out over the water. If you are serious about swimming, drive up to Betterton, which is reputed to have the best swimming beach on the Bay, with a beautiful view and, perhaps more important, no nettles.

Another side trip is the Eastern Neck National Wildlife Refuge, a 2,285-acre park just 6 miles from Rock Hall that is seemingly undiscovered compared with the big names like Assateague and Blackwater. Eastern Neck is actually an island, and you get to it by driving over a tiny log bridge. You can spy on diving and puddle ducks, swans, Canada geese, black duck, and sea ducks like oldsquaw and white-winged scoter. The birds begin arriving in early October and peak in November, mostly departing in April; but herons, egrets, and rails stay around all year. Bald eagles and osprey nest here in this lovely refuge, which is also home to whitetail deer, raccoon, opossum, muskrat, and woodchuck, who love the hedgerows bordering the island roads. End your visit by walking down the boardwalk to an observation deck that looks out over the Bay and affords a wonderful view of the sunset.

Nearby Remington Farms is a wildlife management research and demonstration area laid out on 3,000 acres of what was once the estate of Glenn Martin, the airplane magnate. It's open to the public except in hunting season. The idea is to show how it is possible to upgrade the natural habitat so that both farming and hunting can prosper without decimating wildlife.

Until October this is a Peaceable Kingdom, with ponds and marshes chockablock with mallards and some wood ducks. You tour the place in your car, guided by a leaflet you pick up at the start. The ducks are as unafraid as urban pedestrians and waddle across the road with barely a look at approaching cars.

The White Swan Tavern is at (410) 778-2300; the Imperial Hotel is at (410) 778-5000. For more information, call the Kent County Chamber of Commerce at (410) 778-0416.

EASTON WATERFOWL FESTIVAL

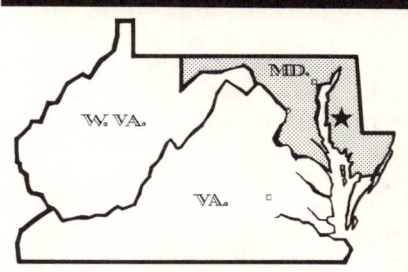

Easton, Maryland, is a town of well under 8,000, settled in 1682, and generally considered the capital of the Eastern Shore. Its citizens are mostly moneyed; there are several real estate dealers and some of the shops have fancy prices. But come the Waterfowl Festival, the type of people in the street seems to change dramatically. The festival brings out the hunters, the locals from nearby who want to see the latest in decoys, ammunition, and gum boots.

On Waterfowl Festival Weekend, usually the second weekend in November, the streets of this old town are bustling with people in camouflage coats, black labradors, small children (and adults) blowing whistles that imitate duck calls, and lovers of water birds inspecting the decoy and painting exhibits in the Tidewater Inn. The Waterfowl Festival is windswept Easton's version of Mardi Gras and it's a wonderful time to visit.

They do it well. The last recorded influx was more than 20,000 visitors, which you would think was impossible for a town this size to absorb. But it works. Buses, sponsored by small arms manufacturer Baretta, bring people into town from parking places on the fringes well-marked with signs, and you can walk almost anywhere you want to go.

Such excitement! A few blocks of Dover and Harrison Streets are blocked off from cars with mini-hay bales speared with geese made out of paper towel roll bodies and plastic heads. The shops on Harrison Street sell antiques and the sort of Eastern Shore items you couldn't find anywhere else—like a 4-foot-tall wooden dog, standing upright and dressed in a hunter's jacket, a rifle slung over his paw. This weekend, the most crowded place is Albright's Gun Shop, but if that's not your interest, you can linger in front of the Tidewater Inn and listen to a fiddle-guitar duo play the "Orange Blossom Special."

In the Gold Room of the Tidewater Inn is a display of waterfowl paintings, including the finalists for the federal duck stamp. (A first edition of the 1971 stamp was on sale in a store across the street, reduced to $1,700.) You can find brass bookends representing eagle heads. Or, have one of the artists photograph your dog during the festival, and he can do a painting from the photo. If art bores you, not to worry: There's a cash bar right in the room with the paintings.

Before you leave the inn, have a look at the remarque boards. A remarque is a bit of original art, usually in pencil, done by an artist to increase the value of a print. All the artists displayed in the Gold Room are invited to "remarque" on two boards that can be seen in a room by the entrance. They have several miniature scenes by different artists—a duck in flight, an eagle head, a boat in marsh grass.

Farther down Harrison Street, you can inspect the electric-motor canoes for sale. If waiting in line doesn't bother you, you ought to see the exhibits at the Armory, where this year's Masterpiece Carving is on display, along with every possible variety of decoy. The year we went, the winner was *Pintails on the Bayou*, an elaborate display of two ducks with their wings spread, flying over marsh grass, the whole scene mounted on a wood platform.

When you're hungry, wander down to Dover and Washington Streets, where you can get oysters on the half shell or crab soup, and a cup of hot chocolate. Settle down at a picnic table and listen to the barbershop quartet, dressed in v-necked sweaters and natty little caps, singing a 1919 favorite, "Baby Won't You Please Come Home?"

Our favorite display was in the Fire Hall, where you can watch the carvers at work and talk to them. The artists are happy to answer questions about what for most of them is a hobby. Mike Smyser, from Manchester, Pennsylvania, a sixth-grade teacher the rest of the week, was operating a simple machine a friend had made him, called a horsehead carving bench. He put a large piece of cork under a light clamp, controlling the pressure with his foot, and shaved off slices of cork until what was left was in the shape of a duck's body. The cedar ducks he makes can also be used for "gunning," as he called it, but the cork models, he said, take more abuse. His dog Teal (as in ducks) sat by patiently while he worked.

Down the hall, Carl Becker used a high speed dentist's drill for carving. He started 22 years ago with a knife and a lot of sandpaper, but soon discovered that electric tools make the carving go much faster. Mr. Becker is a mechanic by trade, but pointed out his daughter Liza across the room and said, "I educated her carving birds," sending her to school on the $31,000 he earned from his hobby.

One of the most popular exhibits is usually the sell-or-swap at the high school. There are, of course, all kinds of decoys: gunning, decorative, hunting. You can get a boxed set of six working decoys, nestled in a wooden box with a waterfowl scene painted on the lid, for $1,800. Antique decoys can be had for $450 apiece.

Then there are the spinoffs, like the porcelain boy doll dressed in army fatigues with a miniature gun and duck over his arm and a sign underneath saying, "Jamie's First Hunt." You can get a free leaflet on "How to Coax Canadas" or videos such as "Calling Canada Geese with Sean Mann and The Eastern Shoreman" or "The Master 'Goose Talk' Championship Videos." (In case you're wondering how best to coax Canadas, Mr. Mann suggests that goose hunters learn these basic calls: the honk or greeting call, the flock or feeding call, the cluck, the murmur, and the whine or cry. The whine or cry can be spelled as "herrowwwwwwwnk.")

Walking around the gym, the basketball hoops above your head, you hear a cacophony of duck calls. Duck-call vendors come from all over to this, the biggest of the country's waterfowl festivals, to hawk their wares. Skip Campbell was there one year from southern Illinois, "where all the ducks are," he said proudly. He explained how the cheaper plastic calls have a brilliant sound, lacking the smooth call of the wood ones.

From there the discussion starts to sound like violinists talking about the making of a Stradivarius. At Skip's booth, you could get a double reed duck call for $40 or a half breed magnum, oiled, for $100. His personal set is made from clarinet-grade cork. The better calls are made from different kinds of wood, from cocobolo (one of the rosebush family) to osage orange.

Skip knew all about the duck calling contest in the high school auditorium that evening. Good calls, he explained, have certain tones and presentations. Although he can recognize a good caller, he said he is not one himself. Apparently it's quite a skill, and he recognizes the limits of his talent.

On the lawn outside the high school was a display with a sign marked "Outlaw Decoys." Being from Washington, I thought it was a boycott action, but it was only the name of a renegade decoy vendor from Spokane, selling decoys that actually fly (they operate on the Bernoulli effect, the same moving air principle that lifts the wings of real birds).

The festival is the brainchild of Dr. Harry Walsh, a local surgeon who, attending a venison festival in Luchow's in New York, decided Easton should capitalize on its water wildlife in the same sort of way. That was in 1971 and things have been snowballing ever since. So many visitors came in 1982 that stocks of the handsome festival catalogue with its fancy photographs ran out.

The Tidewater Inn, of course, is famous. You'd have to be nimble to get overnight reservations during the Waterfowl Festival, but you can eat meals here in style. The dining room has colonial Eastern Shore scenes painted on the wall, and the front lobby is an imposing place with a stone floor, a huge winding spiral staircase, and a fire in the fireplace surrounded by comfortable sofas and winged chairs.

Other places to eat are Yesteryear's, in the Easton Plaza Shopping Center, (410) 822-2433, or the Rustic Inn, at Talbottown and Harrison Streets, (410) 820-8212. The Washington Street Pub has both sandwiches and full dinners.

Wear your gum boots and your earmuffs and buy a catalogue from one of the kiosks. It's an investment in the future. The 1971 catalogue is sold out, and if you could find one, it would probably cost $300.

For Waterfowl Festival information, call (410) 822-4606.

OXFORD, CAMBRIDGE, AND ST. MICHAEL'S

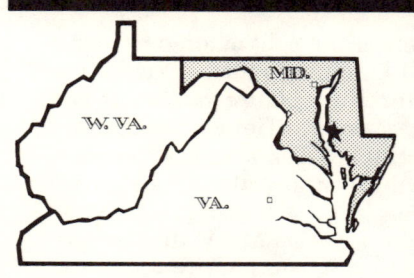

You want to take the Oxford-Cambridge tour in the fall. It's okay in the spring—any place is okay in the spring—but to get the full flavor, go to the Eastern Shore in November after the corn is cropped. The Canada goose is flying south then and the pace of life has quickened beneath their soaring formations. At the Robert Morris Inn in Oxford, Maryland, they are lighting the huge fireplaces to warm the hunters in from their sport. On the shores of the Tred Avon River by the Oxford dock of the little ferry, a woman in a stocking cap stands knee-deep in Canada geese, dispensing bread crusts and hoping the hunters will miss their mark. In the Maritime Museum in St. Michael's, visitors pause to study thoughtfully how their ancestors shot the geese with ancient fowling pieces, how they carved decoys and nearly exterminated the birds before the migratory bird law was enacted.

About 10 miles south of Cambridge, there is even more drama in November. At Blackwater Wildlife Refuge, thousands of Canada geese congregate, winging in low to join their cousins, an early vanguard from the north. The marshes and ponds of Blackwater are alive with the hoarse honking from thousands of black throats, the rustling of wings of thousands of returning wild birds.

If ever there was a time to make the Oxford-Cambridge tour, November is the month. Take the breathtaking slow-measured circuit of Blackwater, walk the ancient brick sidewalks of Oxford, and keep your eyes on the skies. The cry of the wild geese pierces the frosty air as they follow their leaders south on ancient flyway patterns, their long necks silhouetted against the gray of the sky.

Go first to Cambridge and Blackwater and stop at the visitors center to learn something about what you will see. Get a map for Wildlife Drive and study the exhibits so that if you meet an endangered Delmarva squirrel or spot a muskrat den you will recognize it. Leaf through the visitors' book for messages left by earlier bird watchers—"Two bald eagles circling overhead at 10 A.M. Our yearly thrill."

And don't miss the eagle's nest looking like an untidy kindling pile, or the sawed section of ancient loblolly pine whose rings are thumbtacked to pinpoint the history of our country, from the opening of the Panama Canal to the completion of the Alaskan oil pipeline.

Guided by your map you will enter a world belonging to the geese, the eagle, the raccoon—wildlife in many forms. You're encouraged to stay in your car, but unrolling before your eyes is a moving panorama of marshes, dry stubble fields, ponds, and woodland in which every turn of the road is a new discovery. Open your windows and listen to the sounds; absorb an entire landscape covered with Canada geese.

What else you see will depend on how sharp your eyes are and what you are looking for. The slower you go, the more you will see. I spotted blue geese and a great blue heron, dignified and benign as a preacher in a pulpit, his throat feathers ruffling in the wind. Mallard ducks wind in and out of the rushes of the ponds, shore birds dart on the edges of the pond. They are close, far closer than you would expect to see them.

The end of the 6½-mile trail spills you out on the return road to Cambridge and it's time then to head north for Oxford, a charming village on the Tred Avon River where no one hurries and the trees have been leaning over the brick sidewalks for centuries. Oxford is full of modest 18th century houses. Town Creek, on the right as you enter the village, anchors every kind of boat imaginable, masts swaying in the breezes and water slapping their poops.

The big drawing card at Oxford is the Robert Morris Inn, built in 1710 and a well-known hostelry today. The warmth of this country inn envelops you the moment you step in the door. Everything about it is appealing, from the wooden paneling built by long-ago ships' carpenters to the enclosed Elizabethan staircase that leads to the bedrooms above.

Unless you reserve 4 to 6 weeks ahead, (410) 226-5111, you probably will not get to sleep in one of the four-poster beds in these attractive rooms, none of which has telephone or TV. All have their own bath, and all are nonsmoking. Ever since Michener wrote *Chesapeake*, the inn has been packed with guests anxious to take another look at the Eastern Shore. Whether you stay there or not, the inn is happy to feed you, and its crab cakes and oysters are justly famous.

At lunch you'll eat in the tavern wing. The seafood dishes could hardly be fresher and tastier and their reputation has spread, as the out-of-state licenses on the cars outside attest. Afterward you can sit for a spell in the Riverview Room, the inn's parlor overlooking the Tred Avon, where even the most frazzled nerves will unwind. The fireplace there was made from bricks used as ballast in the early sailing days. On the wall is a picture of Robert Morris, Jr., a signer of both the Declaration of Independence and the Constitution. Ken and Wendy Morris have owned the inn more for than 20 years and will take good care of you.

Just outside the windows, the country's oldest ferry not operated by cable has plied the Tred Avon since 1683. Every 20 minutes it docks outside the inn at the landing, scattering Canada geese who are accustomed to handouts on the nearby shore. It can accommodate nine cars and takes you to Bellevue across the river, from which you can reach St. Michael's—worth the trip because of the Maritime Museum on the harbor.

St. Michael's was once a shipbuilding center but now almost all its 1,300 residents are occupied in catching or processing fish. The museum at Navy Point on the waterside reflects the life of the bay, with boat exhibits, an aquarium, and a 12-building museum that has expanded greatly in the last several years.

The museum has the largest floating fleet of historic Chesapeake Bay boats in existence, including a skipjack, log canoe, oyster boat, and crab dredger. There are also decoys, boat building tools, and a small-boat exhibit shed. The latest addition is the steamboat building, highlighting what a museum spokeswoman says is "the only part of the bay's history that was glamorous"—the steamboat era at the turn of the century. You'll see a working steam engine from a bay tugboat, taller than a man, with a huge propeller. Kids can work the boat's telegraph system and light board.

In the same building is a re-created engine shop, with a life-size dummy working on a Model T, his head under the engine. As you approach, a recorded voice, with that distinctive Eastern Shore accent, starts to reminisce about the days when watermen used sailboats instead of the new powerboats. Those were a different breed of boat, he says, but the change is good for him—business is booming now. Mechanics were so few in the early days of the engine that watermen brought all their engines, car and boat, to the same shop.

One of three screw-pile lighthouses from the Chesapeake Bay has been moved here and you should climb the stairs to take a look. All but one of its kind are out of service now, replaced by electronic buoys that surely lack the appeal of this lonely house with its pot-bellied stove, iron bed, and patchwork quilt. You can climb all the way to the top and look out over the water, as well as study the ingenious arrangement of lenses that threw a small light so far to warn ships. And on the way down you can reflect on this entry from the diary (no longer on display) of the lighthouse keeper of another age, separated from his family for all but a couple of weeks every year and lonely on New Year's Eve.

"Usual work at the station," he writes. "Goodbye old year, Your duration has been mingled with sorrows, tears, Heartaches & Joy. Goodbye forever."

As part of its educational program, the Maritime Museum started "Spend the Night in the Lighthouse" for kids, who stay overnight at the lighthouse and do everything the lighthouse keeper did—run the lights and fog bells, and keep shift logs. There's even a surprise middle-of-the-night inspection.

The program was so successful that now adults can do it, too. Grownups also have to bring their own sleeping bags, but they get to go on a cocktail cruise beforehand. Sometimes they have a middle-of-the-night inspection, too. Call (410) 745-2916 for more information about the museum and its programs.

SNOW HILL AND BERLIN

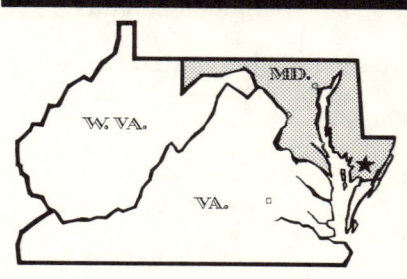

The Eastern Shore has always meant water, but it's more than the Chesapeake Bay. A trip to Snow Hill and Berlin, Maryland, will acquaint you with the pleasures of the Pocomoke River and the Maryland side of Assateague, a jewel of a beach that for some reason is still relatively undiscovered. And if you're in that part of the state, the Nassawango Iron Furnace makes an interesting side trip into a short-lived part of Worcester County's history.

You won't find Snow Hill on any list of Maryland's top tourist attractions; its charms don't scream out. But it has a wonderful river that you can glide down as a passenger, or, if you know your way around canoes, that you can navigate yourself. It has more than 100 buildings over 100 years old, a tiny museum crammed with memorabilia of the town's past, and a couple of good places to eat and spend the night.

To get to Snow Hill from Salisbury, take Snow Hill Road, Route 12, a pleasant road that winds through the Eastern Shore's distinctive flat farmland. The first thing you'll probably want to do when you get to town is explore the river. Go down to Sturgis Park, just off Route 12. You can sit at one of the picnic tables and admire the scenery, and if it's between mid-June and Labor Day, you can take a ride on Tillie the Tug, a 22-passenger boat that makes a leisurely 3-mile journey down the river twice a day.

It feels like a scene from *The Wind in the Willows*; you may even see a river otter. Lynn Lilliston tells you about the river as Tillie wends her way downstream. This is the farthest north that cypress grows naturally on a river (it can be found farther north in swamps), and the Pocomoke has officially been designated a Wild and Scenic River, so no cypress can be removed. Because a lot of the land bordering the water is part of the state park system or The Nature Conservancy preserve, you'll see only five houses in 12 miles of river. It's the deepest river in the United States—estimates range from 30 feet to no limit, where it's fed by an underground spring.

The Pocomoke—Algonquin for "dark water"—is colored by the tannic acid from the cypress, but the water is clean. The sailing ships that plied the river until the end of World War II used to stock up on the Pocomoke's water for long sea voyages, taking advantage of tannic acid's preservative qualities.

In its day, the Pocomoke hid bootleggers and members of the Underground Railroad. Now, it sports blue herons, bald eagles, cormorants, and kingfishers. Wild rice that predates the Civil War grows in one inlet, and red belly and painted turtles like to sun themselves on their favorite log, sometimes 23 crowded on top of each other. There's even a peacock who perches on a tree on Goat Island, flying across the river at lunchtime to visit the picnickers. Lynn, the boat's narrator, thinks he needs a girlfriend; judging from his eager response to Tillie's whistle, he seems to think the tug is his best chance.

The Pocomoke is known for its bass fishing. If you'd like to try your hand at it, the Pocomoke River Canoe Company rents canoes, kayaks, pontoons, and motorboats. But be forewarned: It's a tidal river, so the current can be strong. Those less experienced might want to go upriver, where there are no power boats and there's less of a current.

The Canoe Company is worth visiting for another reason: the train museum upstairs. Barry Laws, who works at the bank across the street during the week and at the Canoe Company on weekends, spent his spare time with a couple of friends putting together a model train that runs all around the large attic room, complete with details like the Snow Hill depot and the town's old lumber warehouse. Before a road was cleared to Chincoteague, the train used to go to Franklin City, Virginia, and carry oysters and clams from Chincoteague up to the Northeast. The station, built in the late 1800s, still stands today. A freight train runs from Philadelphia, hauling grain for the feed mills and ending at Snow Hill. During Heritage Weekend, the third weekend in October, you can ride an excursion train from Snow Hill to Berlin.

The Julia A. Purnell Museum on Market Street, housed in an old church, is filled with the possessions of this remarkable Snow Hill resident, who lived to be more than 100 and took up needlepoint at age 80, when she suddenly found herself in a wheelchair after an injury. Her stitching won her a place in the Hobby Hall of Fame at age 99. When she died, her son William was left with a houseful of her needlework and collections of various bits of Americana, which he gave to the town.

In one display case that tells the history of Worcester County from the Stone Age to the future, you can find Indian arrowheads, the smallest Bible ever made (it looks like it, and who is to contradict this?), a sign for a $2,400 reward for a runaway slave, and at the end, a shutter covering a mirror, to show the future. A section in the back has so much in it—an old typewriter, duck decoys, lace-up shoes, an 1895 receipt from a Baltimore store—that it is labeled "T.M. Purnell General Merchandise." The objects represent the customs of another era, making it seem so long ago: a lady's spittoon, Miss Julia's silver carrying card cases, her black mourning jewelry, and a rotating shoo-fly fan.

You can also learn a little about the history of the town here. It was declared a Royal Port of Entry in 1694 because it was slightly elevated and surrounded by fertile forests. You can see photos of steamboats that plied the Pocomoke on the way to Baltimore and of the lumber mill that dominated the town in the late 1800s. The steam whistle that announced the shift changes is displayed.

Snow Hill is the kind of place where you can spend a pleasant afternoon walking along the brick sidewalks lined with century-old sycamores, enjoying the sense of peace, and admiring the old homes. (Federal Street in particular has many houses from the 19th century.) You may, as we did, see the mayor, a retired Foreign Service officer, mowing the lawn of his rambling old Victorian house. He lives in a house built by a former governor of Maryland, John Walter Smith, known earlier in his career as the free book senator because of his legislation to provide free textbooks to Maryland students.

You can eat and stay at the Snow Hill Inn, (410) 632-2102, whose original ownership dates to 1793. It has a lovely back garden with a gazebo and a patio with a couple of tables. The dining room decor, like the food, isn't fancy, tending toward golden oak and (naturally) crab cakes. Owner and chef Jim Washington says his goal is to present a menu where nothing has to be explained. Like the rest of the town, it's a comfortable and pleasant place.

For more elegant accommodations, there is the Chanceford Hill Inn, (410) 632-2231; a third choice is the River House Inn, (410) 632-2722.

About 5 miles north of Snow Hill on Route 12 is a re-creation of a type you won't often find: the company town from an old iron works. The Nassawango Iron Furnace was only active for 30 years before it apparently disappeared into the earth. Although a very imposing chimney remains standing, the ironmaster's mansion seems to have disappeared without a trace and without explanation. It is almost eerie to go to Furnace Town on a summer Saturday afternoon and find it more silent than a nature preserve—especially when you try to envision a roaring furnace going night and day.

There were high hopes for the Nassawango Furnace when it began operation in the early 1830s. An editorial from the *Snow Hill Messenger* for May 21, 1832, titled "Improvement in

Worcester," captures the feeling of faith in the Industrial Revolution. A few months earlier, the writer says, the area had been "a rugged forest." But now, it employs 60 people and extracts "a large quantity of fine iron ore" from the earth. "As citizens of Worcester we feel much indebted to those enterprising strangers who have erected an iron furnace in our county and fondly hope it will prove of considerable advantage to themselves in a pecuniary point of view."

But the furnace only gave its pecuniary advantage until about 1850. At first, it was an innovation because it was one of the early hot blast furnaces, with a system of connecting pipes that raised the temperature inside dramatically and speeded up the whole process. The iron monster required a lot of stoking: When the furnace was running, every 2 hours men would shovel and dump 500 pounds of bog ore, 40 pounds of shells, and 25 bushels of charcoal into the furnace. After the 1840s, the Nassawango Furnace couldn't compete on the national market, especially with the new iron works opening in the Great Lakes region.

Today, in addition to the large stack of the iron furnace, you can see a blacksmith shop, a church, a broom house, and print shop. All the buildings have been brought in from elsewhere because when the Worcester County Historical Society began restoration in the 1970s, all that remained was the furnace stack and a few overgrown foundations. Although the property now has many tall trees, there were none when the furnace was operating because they were all cut down to make charcoal.

If you really want to immerse yourself in Furnace Town's past, join one of the supervised excavations on a Sunday in the summer. Nails, glass bottles, and pipe bowls have been found in past digs and are displayed in the blacksmith shop. Reservations are needed; call (410) 632-2032.

After trying to imagine the bustle and noise of the furnace's heyday, you can enjoy the quiet of today and take the mile-long nature trail kept by The Nature Conservancy on the lower part of the property. You'll go through a cypress swamp and upland woods and for part of the way follow the path of the old furnace canal, used to transport the iron ore to ships in the Nassawango Creek. Today, it's occupied by hummingbirds, prickly-pear cactus, and jewelweed. Watch for the cypress "knees," small growths alongside the trunk that come out of the tree's root system.

There are two main reasons to go to Berlin (pronounced BURR-lin): to eat at the Atlantic Hotel and because it's on the way to Assateague. The Atlantic Hotel, built in 1895, had a checkered history after its life as a hotel ended the first time in 1939. It was, at various points, a brothel, soda fountain, real estate office, dry goods store, and martial arts studio. Luckily for us, in 1984, when it became clear that the hotel was going to fall down or be torn down, 10 local businessmen got together and bought it. A massive amount of restoration was required, but the Atlantic opened its doors again in 1988.

When the Atlantic Hotel was built by Horace F. Harmonson, it accommodated traveling salesmen, known as "drummers." Livestock sales were held in the livery stable in back of the hotel. Today, it's just a parking lot, from which you can look up to the second floor porch, furnished with chairs for the guests. Inside, there's a parlor with Victorian furniture. The doors, woodwork, and stained glass were all restored and reinstalled for the 1988 reopening. The rooms are a little rococo, but reasonably priced, and all have their own bath.

But the real news at the Atlantic is in the dining room. It serves excellent French-influenced food, and you are likely to find local seafood among the specials. The Sunday brunch is a bargain. For more casual fare, you can go to the hotel's Drummer Cafe, which includes an outdoor terrace.

Berlin has several antique shops, nearly all closed on Sunday. The Tumbling Monkeys Gift Shop, 120 North Main Street, sells imaginatively painted furniture: stools painted to look like watermelon, a coffee table with a *trompe l'oeil* fishpond.

My favorite—and it is open Sunday—is the Globe bookstore. Not only is it a nice little store with some unusual books on the Eastern Shore, but it also has an upstairs gallery of jewelry, prints, and pottery, plus an antique and second-hand shop. The Globe was a theater in the early part of the century, showing acts like the Del-Mar-Va Magician, for which an old ad hangs in the women's room: "7th season active in Magic, Presenting ALL NEW, a program of 'ESCAPE MYSTERIES' including the famous 'SACK ESCAPE'...Bring Your OWN Padlocks."

The Globe now has occasional folk concerts in the old theater and also has a small cafe with gourmet coffees, teas, and sandwiches.

If you want to explore Berlin further, you can pick up a self-guided walking tour brochure at the Globe that will tell you about the town's two centuries of architectural heritage. There are several 19th century homes with wonderful big porches. It's enjoyable just to walk along the sycamore-lined streets after a meal at the Atlantic Hotel.

Of course if you get as far as Berlin, you will surely go on to Assateague, only a few miles farther to the coast. You will likely not be going to Ocean City, which is about the same distance, if you are the kind of person who likes quiet places like Berlin and

124   Snow Hill. Everything that Ocean City is, Assateague isn't, and that to me is Assateague's chief advantage.

The Maryland side of Assateague (the Virginia side is near Chincoteague) is part Maryland state park and part national park. Mostly, Assateague is just miles of beach unspoiled by boardwalks, pizza joints, or video games. And you may well see some of the wild ponies made famous by Marguerite Henry's book for children, *Misty of Chincoteague*. Once you're there, sitting in traffic on the Bay Bridge seems a small sacrifice.

Tillie the Tug can be reached at (301) 632-0680 or (800) 345-6754. For reservations at the Atlantic Hotel, call (301) 641-3589.

LAND OF THE CRABBER, OYSTERMAN & FARMER

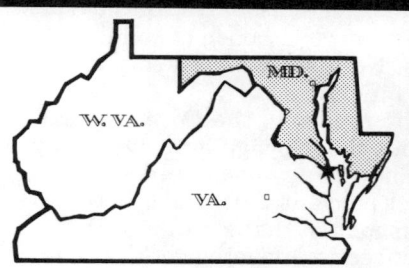

Every weekend the cars pour across the Bay Bridge headed for the ocean beaches, bumper to bumper in their haste to put all or most of Maryland behind them. The sandy stretches of the Atlantic shores are the target and, perhaps because of this, the southern part of the Free State remains an overlooked watery world sleeping in the shadow of the better known Eastern Shore.

St. Mary's County, mother of Maryland, is a land designed not for swimming but for boating. Its shores, innocent of vacation resorts, are dotted with plantations once owned by towering early Maryland figures, and its past is heavy with the history of the state's beginnings. This is the land of the crabber, the oysterman, and the farmer, evoking a simpler era. If you do not know St. Mary's County, you have missed a whole fascinating world.

The first capital of Maryland was here in St. Mary's City, which is not a city at all but a tiny cluster of buildings. Leonard Calvert and his little band of Englishmen landed here in 1634 in the *Ark* and the *Dove*, seeking to establish a colony where Catholicism would be not frowned upon. A replica of the *Dove* rides at anchor at the foot of the bluff; a reconstruction of the first State House has been built on the original site; and an ancient cannon points its muzzle over the harbor. Close by, Trinity Church, a johnny-come-lately built in 1828, lifts its spire to the sky above an old graveyard. That's St. Mary's City.

During the 350th anniversary of the founding of "St. Marie's Cittie," the state of Maryland added a 17th century inn known as Farthing's Ordinary and a typical tobacco plantation belonging to a mythical Godiah Spray. These were constructed only with tools available in the day and even the tobacco growing in the Spray fields, planted to cater to the new fad for the weed in England, remains true to the time.

But the fun of it all is the way in which the history of the place reaches out to involve the visitor, spilling out from the handful of simple frame houses built on the grassy land behind the State House door.

Stroll out behind the State House to look at the cannon and, like as not, a young man in colonial costume will pluck your elbow. "And what do you be thinkin' about the price of tobacco this year?" he will inquire. And there you are, transported right into the thick of 1685. You might be asked to help find an indentured servant who has run away, or even to serve as a juror in the trial of John Coode, a Protestant rabble-rouser accused of collaborating with Canada and the Indians. No history book will put you in touch with the 17th century so quickly.

Down on the river below is the replica of the *Dove*. You can board it and learn something about that voyage long ago. They do a marvelous job of explaining how things were, and you'll be struck again and again what quiet nerve it must have taken to entrust yourself to the Atlantic's moods in that small vessel.

In the next few years, a new section devoted to American Indian culture will be added behind the visitors center. Maize and sassafras will be planted. You'll be able to learn about the tattoos the Indians used—different for men and women, and for different occupations—by putting your hand under a transparent piece of plastic to see how it would look with a tattoo. A bow will be strung so non-archers can feel what it's like to pull it back as the Indians would have (sorry, no arrows). You will be able to look through an eyepiece and see a vision of a deer as a hunter would have.

The Great Brick Chapel from the 1660s is also being reconstructed, and visitors can come and watch its progress during the summer excavation season. No trace of 17th century St. Mary's City is visible above ground, so archeological evidence is all historians have to go on: The cross-shaped foundation of the brick chapel has already been discovered, and excavators are working to uncover the remains of a wooden Catholic chapel from 1634. Archeologists are also searching for the fort built by colonists when they first came to Maryland seeking tolerance for their Catholic faith. In 25 years of excavating, they have yet to find the fort. "It's so big we could easily miss it," says a spokeswoman for Historic St. Mary's City—an interesting thought.

When the chapels are brought to the surface, visitors will be able to go through an exhibit about religious tolerance. In the 17th century, of course, the Catholics meant this to apply only to Christians, not to American Indians.

St. Mary's City made the news in 1990 when three lead coffins were found in the Great Brick Chapel. After much research and planning, they were lifted out three years later (on Friday the 13th) without disturbing the remains—no easy task. Because the coffins were made of lead, a good preservative, historians hoped to find mummies inside them. They didn't, but they did find samples of flesh, hair, and clothing—all rare for the 17th century.

When the state capital moved to Annapolis, St. Mary's City failed because it had no other economic base. It was a planned city laid out in connecting triangles—a sophisticated idea that had not yet been tried in the New World. Unfortunately, the plan didn't get off the ground after the capital was moved.

St. Mary's County offers several handsome plantation homes, and perhaps the jewel of them all is Sotterley. Just 60 miles from downtown Washington, Sotterley sits on a hillside near Hollywood, Maryland, overlooking the Patuxent River. Sotterley, a graceful survivor from the 18th century, is open to the public, and a stroll through it is like a visit to a country home whose host is absent, perhaps because it has always been lived in and used since its beginnings in 1727.

For almost three centuries Sotterley's owners have looked down from the long veranda on the Patuxent River and a flock of sheep like those that still graze on the hillside below. Country hams hang in the smokehouse as they always have, and you can buy some slices or a whole one to take home. In the corn crib a succession of cats has been born, the last still strolling the paths underneath the rose-covered trellises.

James Bowles, an Englishman of means, built Sotterley. His widow married George Plater, in whose family it remained for several generations until, as legend has it, the last of the Platers gambled Sotterley away in a dice game in the red-walled library. For the next nearly 100 years Sotterley belonged to the Briscoes, whose ancestors arrived on the *Dove* and its sister ship, the *Ark*. In 1910 it was bought by Herbert Satterlee, who restored it to its original elegance.

It was the early Platers who turned the house from a simple plantation home into a mansion. Most of the work was done by indentured servants, especially by Richard Boulton, who carved the famous Chippendale staircase and the shell alcoves in the drawing room, which to this day is only candlelit. One story has it that on the day his term as bonded servant was over, he picked up his tools and walked off a free man, leaving behind a tiny piece of molding in the staircase still unfinished.

Pirates are said to have attacked Sotterley, so handy from the river, planning the attack for the daytime when they thought the men would be at work in the fields. But a hunt breakfast was in progress at the mansion and the riders routed the brigands. Secret loose panels and a passageway hidden in a closet attest to the fact that a hasty escape was never very far from the occupants' minds.

The bell in the William Cummens clock on the landing is thought to have been made by Paul Revere, and the windowpanes, at least in the library, are the 18th century originals. The rugs in this room are Jail Agra, rugs Queen Victoria ordered to keep Moslem prisoners busy while serving sentence for refusing to grease cannon balls with pork fat.

The floors at Sotterley undulate gently with the warp of centuries, but this seems only the charming foible of an aging beauty. The house is open and cool, always filled with flowers from the truly magnificent cutting gardens that stretch endlessly in the sunlight. To this day Sotterley is the setting for elegant parties, for it is rented out for weddings and lunches to those who want a truly old world air for their festivities.

St. Mary's City, Sotterley, and Solomons Island, at the tip of Calvert County across the Patuxent, form a triangle that can be managed in a day's trip from Washington, although an overnight stay in one of the bed and breakfasts or budget motels makes it a more leisurely junket.

In any case, don't miss Solomons, where the best area seafood restaurants are and where you can get a feel for the biology of the bay in the Calvert Marine Museum. Take the Governor Thomas Johnson Memorial Bridge across the river (it's well-marked off Route 4 below Hollywood), and turn right off the bridge for the museum. You can't miss it because of Drum Point Lighthouse, clearly visible from the road and looking for all the world like a cozy cottage on stilts.

The history of oystering in the bay is all laid out in the J.C. Lore Oyster House, half a mile south of the main museum complex on Route 2. When the 1934 seafood packing house closed in the late 1960s, the museum acquired it, along with its records and equipment. The shucking room and canning equipment are as the last owners left them. Exhibits tell the history and traditions of the region's commercial finfish, crab, oyster, eel, and clam fisheries. A boat-building exhibit on the second floor explains how wooden workboats are built today. If you like model boats, there's a woodcarving and model boat shop where you can see a master woodcarver and model-maker at work. There's even a marsh walk and a boat basin where museum staff demonstrate oyster tonging and crab pot and fishing techniques.

The discovery room is fun no matter what your age. You can sift through a sandbox and find fossilized shark's teeth, just as you might at Calvert Cliffs up the shore. The museum staff will help you identify which kind of shark it came from and mount it on a card for you to take home.

Paleontology is one of the themes of the museum, since 20 million years ago this part of Maryland was under water and Great White Sharks ruled the territory. The museum is building a 45-foot skeleton of one, big as a tour bus, based on research that staff members did in South Africa. You can walk through it while it's under construction and ask questions of the people building it. It's scheduled to be finished in 1996.

In 1992, the museum opened a 15-tank estuarium that has everything from an oyster bar to one of the few jellyfish tanks in the country. The museum covers life along the Patuxent River as well as activity in the bay.

They say the ghost of a young girl inhabits the cupola of the lighthouse, keeping company with the lens upstairs and occasionally opening doors that were left locked the night before. If so, it must get windy and lonely up there—but at least she doesn't have to endure the loud ring of the 1,400 pound bell, which hasn't been rung for several years.

This screw-pile lighthouse is one of only three such cottage types remaining on the bay. The lighthouse is the only part of the museum not accessible to the handicapped (its historic status prevents it from being modified), but a new video will follow a tour guide around the lighthouse with a camera, for those who can't get in on their own. The video will also describe the monumental job of moving it here to the museum from its original location at Drum Point.

One of the very nicest things you can do in Solomons is to take the river cruise in the *Wm. B. Tennison*. She's a bugeye whose bottom was built from only nine mammoth logs, somewhat in the fashion of a dugout canoe, though she has a comfortable superstructure and an awning to keep the sun off part of the deck. She steams out to the bridge at 2 P.M. for an hour's ride from Wednesday to Sunday from May to October, and nothing could be more pleasant than watching the shoreline slip slowly by as she moves out like a respectable mother hen among the fly-by-night small pleasure craft.

A representative from the museum goes along to answer questions and point out the osprey nests where feathered broods of youngsters are being fledged. The nests look like an untidy pile of sticks thrown into the channel marker where they are perched, but osprey mothers look down with enormous dignity on curious passersby. The departure is from the museum dock.

The big treat of a southern Maryland adventure is, of course, the fish, which has to be as fresh as any you will ever have. Both The Captain's Table and the Lighthouse Inn serve every variety of finny fare in nice dining rooms overlooking the water. You can eat your soft-shelled crab and watch a family of geese making their way across the water in hopes of a handout, mother and father convoying the goslings with sober solicitude.

The mallards here are as greedy as city pigeons and swarm around the harbor police when its crew docks for a restorative cup of coffee.

If the museum exhibits and the boat trip make you hungry to see more of the area's natural beauty firsthand, you can visit two state parks in Calvert County: Battle Creek Cypress Swamp and Flag Ponds Nature Park. Battle Creek contains one of the northernmost naturally occurring stands of bald cypress trees in the country; an elevated boardwalk takes you through the thick of them. It is a swamp, though, so be sure and bring plenty of insect repellent. It's open year-round except Mondays and major holidays. Flag Ponds has 3 miles of easy hiking trails, observation platforms overlooking two ponds, a wetlands boardwalk, a beach and fishing pier on the bay, and a visitors center. It is open every day in the summer and weekends the rest of the year. Call (410) 535-5327 or (800) 331-9771 for information about both parks.

Historic St. Mary's City is open from 10 A.M. to 5 P.M. Wednesday through Sunday from the end of March through November; call (301) 862-0990. Sotterley is open from 11 A.M. to 4 P.M. daily except Monday from June through October and by appointment in April, May, November, and December; call (301) 373-2280. Calvert Marine Museum is open 10 A.M. to 5 P.M. year-round except major holidays. Call (410) 326-2042 to check hours of Drum Point Lighthouse and J.C. Lore Oyster House.

WEST VIRGINIA

The road signs in West Virginia really do say Wild Wonderful West Virginia, and they don't exaggerate. Some of the loveliest unspoiled land within range of the capital city is in the Mountain State. The hills and turns there have not been made to bow to the road grader, and roads wander through the countryside with a mind of their own. The Mountain State is beautiful.

It started life as part of Virginia, but the Commonwealth didn't pay much attention to its western citizens, and they took umbrage. Right in the middle of the Civil War, West Virginia became the 35th state. West (by God) Virginia is what the natives call it.

It's mountainous. Spruce Knob in Pendleton County is 4,862 feet high. Three-quarters of the state is forest covered. It's a shunpiker's dream and its rugged past left it dotted with towns with names like Cutlips, Left Hand, and Elk Forest, not to mention Nettie. The terrain is so rough that the Indians didn't settle there, content to use it only for hunting and fishing.

In fall, the fields are yellow with mustard and yarrow; in spring, the state flower, the rhododendron, covers the roadside. Red-wing blackbirds adorn the fence posts, black bear are not unheard of in the forest preserves, deer and wild turkey call the leafy glades home. West Virginia is the most western feeling of our eastern states, retaining still the look of how it was before the coming of cement and asphalt.

At Harpers Ferry the Civil War is part of everyday life, recreated in living history, and John Brown's fort still stands where it did when he hatched his abolitionist plot. In Berkeley Springs, the baths where George Washington once lowered his tall frame are still in operation. On the steep slopes of Cheat Mountain, a Shay steam engine still makes the climb to the top as it did in the early logging days. Progress is held at bay in West Virginia.

When you buy apples or cider at the roadside stands or gas at the mom-and-pop's, take time to visit with the people who sell to you. This part of the world is not homogenized by TV and the movies, and from these hardy and independent folk you'll get the flavor of life in the state whose motto is Mountaineers are Always Free. This is a piece of the east not yet tamed, spared by its rugged topography.

West Virginia—it's high on my list of favorite places, and it's just the other side of the river.

HARPERS FERRY

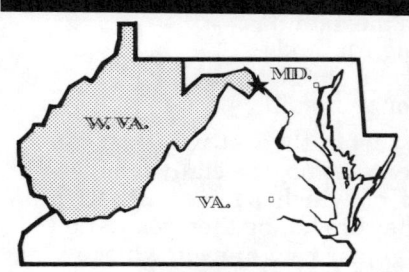

November is voting month, but not in Harpers Ferry, West Virginia, where the vote is in October. It's Election Day 1860, and you can cast your ballots after hearing the candidates debate. The hated Republican candidate Abraham Lincoln is not on the ballot in this southern state (Harpers Ferry was part of Virginia then), and—a concession to modernity—women are allowed to vote.

You will hear speeches by electors for Stephen Douglas, John Bell, and John Breckinridge. Wearing top hats and white gloves, they point their canes at the audience for emphasis and refer to their opponents as "namby-pamby weak-kneed men." (The political rhetoric was on no higher plane then, but the vocabulary was apparently more colorful.)

The memory of John Brown's raid on the Armory the year before is still fresh. "For 36 hours, we were terrified the Civil War was at our doors," says a woman in a hoop skirt. She describes the ill-fated man's hanging: "John Brown's body sways between heaven and earth." Harpers Ferry is an industrial community of more than 3,000 people including 300 African Americans, half of whom are slaves. "When you pull that lever to vote," we are told, "you may be deciding that we will go to war." (No one was pulling levers to vote in 1860, but that's a quibble.)

Electors sing campaign songs to the tune of "Yankee Doodle" and walk the streets bearing placards and pressing campaign literature on you. The streets, from which cars have been banned, are filled with women wearing hoop skirts and carrying parasols, their hair gathered in crocheted nets.

After the political speeches under the tent, the women take the floor to urge temperance on the audience. One abandoned wife sobs out a story of her drunkard husband leaving his family in the lurch. A gentleman who has been converted to the cause offers a moving rendition of "Oh Father, Oh Father, Please Come Home." A placard at the front traces the progress from temperance to intemperance, starting with water, moving to milk and water, through small beer, punch, toddy and egg rum, bitters and cordials, drams in the morning, and ending with continual drinking. A list of vices, diseases, and punishment accompanies each stage.

134   The audience is invited to join the Temperance ladies in singing the anthem of Temperance Lodge #72:

> For our country and our families,
> We will fight King Alcohol!
> Come our brothers! Come our sisters!
> For Cold Water conquers all!

But don't worry, if you're still part of the wet vote, you can go next door to a tavern that has been set up especially for Election Day (one wonders on behalf of which party). Although women who enter are warned that they are taking their reputation in their hands, they can still order ginger beer or even whiskey.

Election Day is a busy time. While the Temperance ladies are testifying, you can hear the militia marching down the street behind you. They take a couple of turns around the town in smart formation, while the candidates' representatives watch from the reviewing stand. Don't forget to cast your ballots at the dry goods store, and if you stay till the end, you'll be able to hear the results and watch the victory parade.

Election Day is usually the second Saturday in October, but if you stay over, you can see the rest of the town that abolitionist John Brown put in the pages of history. Attractive to both nature and history buffs, the town is in a beautiful setting, and several museums and displays are within easy walking distance of each other in the town, much of which is a national park.

You park your car in a lot above the town a couple of miles away, and a shuttle bus drops you off near the visitors center, originally a stagecoach inn built in the 1820s, now run by the Park Service. Park rangers there can answer your questions and give you maps of nature trails, ranging from small trails around town to hardy hikes on the Appalachian Trail. Some trails are suitable for strollers. The center also has a good bookstore with a lot of Civil War material and a good section on black history.

After that, the dry goods store where you voted is a good place to start. Built in 1812, the building was the home of the master armorer until 1858. Today, it is filled with a variety of wares that you would have to search for all over the mall in the 1990s: tinware, medicine, produce, rakes, cribs, brandy, shirts and collars, and hoops for your skirts. An 1850 price list is helpfully provided: You could buy sheets of writing paper at 2 cents each, a live hen for a dollar, or patent medicine for killing worms, 25 cents. Costumed volunteers can answer your questions. They would have played a vital role in the store's heyday because nothing was self-serve.

You'll also find men in costume at the provost marshall's

office next door. The Union provost guard, the enforcer of military rule, patrolled the streets of Harpers Ferry during the Civil War, demanding that citizens show their passes. During 4 years of Civil War, Harpers Ferry changed hands eight times.

From June through Labor Day, you can take a guided tour of the town with a park ranger on any of five themes: industry (mostly the Armory and other water power), John Brown, the Civil War, African American history, and natural history. Whether or not you go on the John Brown tour, you will want to trace the footsteps of Brown and his men, stopping at his fort and the Armory fire engine house, now resting almost where it originally stood, after having been moved five times. Once it went to Chicago as a paid attraction, but just 11 people paid, so they brought it home on a flatcar, right up Route 340, to the place where it had originally stood. Its failure as an exhibit was probably slated anyway, but to make matters worse, the people in Chicago had reassembled it from a negative when it arrived in pieces, so they put everything together backward.

The engine house looks at home in Harpers Ferry, and it now houses the very fire engine that shared the fort with Brown and his men on that 1859 October night. The door on which Robert E. Lee (then a colonel) beat to demand Brown's surrender has been removed to the John Brown Museum, where exhibits tell the whole story of the raid.

Brown and his 22-man army actually succeeded in seizing the town's armory before the surprised citizenry knew what was happening. He was captured and brought to trial, sentenced to death as he lay on a litter, weak from a gunshot wound. A couple months later he was hanged at nearby Charles Town. You can walk through his life and death in the town wax museum.

One of Harpers Ferry's big industries until 1861 was gun making. The Armory here was the southern counterpart of the U.S. Armory at Springfield, Massachusetts. You can see the remains of the arsenal where they stored the guns and what's left of the scarred muskets after federal soldiers burned the building in 1861. At the restored master armorer's house, you can learn the story of gun making.

Robert Harper knew what he was doing when he built his house on the hill high above the two rivers. The town sits at the confluence of the mighty Shenandoah and Potomac Rivers, and the clearing of riverbank forests brought frequent flooding. The flood of 1870 wiped out much of the town's industry, and the 1936 flood brought water to the second-story level of buildings along Shenandoah Street. You can see the high-water mark of the floods in displays near the Village Green. In 1936 the river rose 36 feet, which may account for the exposed tree roots running like ghostly fingers toward the river beyond.

A relatively new exhibit, on High Street, is Black Voices from Harpers Ferry. You can see a thick cow-skin whip that was used to whip slaves and learn how some local slave owners earned extra income by renting their slaves to the U.S. government—something historians found out from the Armory slave roll. At several stands, you can pick up a phone and hear the stories of individual slaves—like Isaac Gilbert, a slave who raised $1,400 to buy his wife and three children. But since property couldn't buy property, he could do nothing until he got the help of Fontaine Beckham, the mayor of Harpers Ferry.

In 1806, the Virginia General Assembly decided no free black could remain in the state more than a year without reverting to slavery. Things were not much better by the time of the Civil War, when thousands of slaves came to Harpers Ferry. There was a Union garrison here where runaway slaves came for refuge. Only about a third of the slaves in the town were men. The rest were women and children working as laundresses, cooks, housekeepers, and servants.

When the burden of human history presses down on you, climb the worn stone steps from High Street, past St. Peter's Church with its imposing steeple, to Jefferson Rock. From there, you will see one of the most spectacular views you could hope for. Thomas Jefferson thought so; when he visited in 1783, he called it "worth a voyage across the Atlantic." You can see three states (West Virginia, Virginia, and Maryland), the Shenandoah River on your right, the Potomac on your left, and tree-covered hills all around.

On the way back to High Street, stop at Robert Harper's house, built in the 1770s and now the oldest surviving structure in the park. Both George Washington and Jefferson probably dined in the house, which was made into a tavern on his death. You'll see it today as it was when James McGraw rented it in the mid-19th century for $60 annually, climbing those steps every night after a day of selling whiskey, coffee, horse muzzles, bee smokers (protective devices used by beekeepers), and horseshoe nails in the general store on Shenandoah Street.

If you want to eat in town, two places on High Street—the Mountain House Cafe and the Garden of Food—have pleasant outdoor patios where you can sit if the weather is good. The Garden of Food has a nice inside room, too, with stone and wood paneling. You can even drink a West Virginia wine, Breeder's Reserve from Schneider's Winery.

For dinner with a panoramic view, drive about a mile out of town to the Hilltop House, an old-fashioned hotel that sits high above the town. It's a country hotel and while it now has 66 rooms and air conditioning, it has kept its old-time flavor from the days when it was a favorite of Mark Twain and Woodrow Wilson. You can eat everything from pheasant or venison to curry chicken mousse, and then take your ease in a rocking chair on the veranda.

For information, call the Harpers Ferry Information Center, (304) 535-6029. If you decide to go other than Election Day or during the summer months, the living history staff is smaller and not always all in costume. The shuttle bus from the satellite parking lots runs all year round from 7:30 A.M. to 6 P.M.

SHEPHERDSTOWN

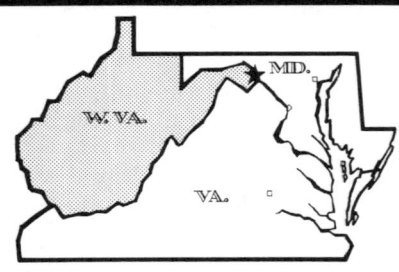

The little girl eating the German chocolate bar is wearing a button that says, "Kiss Me, I'm Irish," but she's in the minority. All around her are people wearing Tyrolean hats, suspender-held walking shorts, peasant dresses with aprons, and stout boots. The band is playing the Heidelberg drinking song. It's Octoberfest in Shepherdstown, West Virginia, and the accent is Bavarian.

The Bavarian Inn puts on the festival annually on the third Sunday of September to honor Shepherdstown's German heritage and that of innkeeper Aram Asam. Asam and his English wife, Carol, have made the old greystone mansion bought in 1962 into an inn that is a little bit of Germany transplanted. Their menu features the dishes of Asam's native Munich, and the outlying guest chalets are as Alpine as if they overlooked the Danube instead of the Potomac.

Repeat visitors to the festival are knowledgeable: they know the polka, the schottische, and the words to the German songs. And they come dressed for the part. From the silver-haired couple circling the floor to the "Beer Barrel Polka," to the young father dancing with a daughter so small he lifts her feet off the ground, the crowd really enters into the spirit.

Lines for the food (and the beer) get long, but the festive crowd doesn't seem to mind. There's plenty to distract the eye, like the 1923 band organ playing under a tree with splendid padded mechanical clowns bowing and turning to the pretend music they play, mesmerizing the children.

If you hate alfresco dining, you can take your food in the dining room on a first-come, first-serve basis, no reservations. But just outside, on the natural slope of the hill, is as fine a place as you can imagine to picnic and watch, from your high vantage point, the dancers kicking up their heels to the music of the tuba, the fiddle, and the squeeze box played by the Edelweiss band. A clown, busy blowing up balloons, attracts the children, and the view of the river stretches out into the distance like the backdrop of a stage set. From the tables of the vendors you can buy German black bread and local crafts, like the Maryland flag done in stained glass or the handmade wooden bird feeders—and, of course, beer steins. They're displayed under signs saying, "You never sausage prices." It's all good Alpine fun.

Beyond the fences of the Bavarian Inn is Shepherdstown itself, a 1732 town that claims it's the oldest in the state. It was here, in 1787, that James Rumsey launched the first steamboat, and you can walk down to the monument marking the spot. (From German Street, turn left just before the railroad tracks.) It's an odd sort of thing, a very tall Ionic column topped by a globe—but when you climb up the steps and lean over its railing, you're treated to a beautiful view of the river and the hills. You might even see a train chugging across the railroad bridge, sporting the motto, "Southern serves the South."

Be sure to stop at the Historic Shepherdstown Museum in the old Entler Hotel. Originally built in 1786, but diminished by a fire in 1912, what you now see dates to 1790 and 1809. After its days as a grand hotel, it became a men's dorm at Shepherd College in the 1920s. Scheduled for demolition in 1971, the townspeople protested so vociferously that it was saved and placed on the National Register of Historic Places.

Today it holds all sorts of wonderful local memorabilia, from the Penmanship Drill Book of 1898, admonishing the writer to "Get Wisdom: Go to the ant thou slugg and Delay not," to the invitation posted upstairs:

> Dance and Supper at the Entler Hotel
> You are politely invited to attend
> Music: Jack's Band
> May 15, 1879

Upstairs is a room furnished as it would have been in the Entler's glory days, with a metal foot warmer that held live charcoal, a metal hip bath used in front of the fireplace, and on the stencilled wall, a sampler made by Shepherdstown resident Mary Swagler in 1833 reads,

> Oh Mary think of me when I am gone
> I will think of thee till it is done.

A few miscellaneous artifacts are lacking in historical detail, though still of interest. The label for some American Indian arrowheads and tools, for example, reads, "8,000-1,500 BP (Before the Present). All found in the immediate area of Shepherdstown. Tribe or tribes unknown." Across the hall, a large wooden object's note requests, "Your Guess. Silage cutter or straw cutter for making brooms. If you can give us a definitive answer, please do."

Be sure and see the half-scale replica of Rumsey's steamboat in the back shed. The first time it was put on the water, it sank, but we were assured by the proud proprietors of the museum that there's going to be another try. Behind the museum, there's a nice back porch with a swing, if you're ready for a rest.

Shepherdstown's main street, German Street, offers several interesting little shops. Dickinson's Pottery Studio and Crafts Gallery has unusual pottery and elaborately dipped candles, and The Shaman's Shop has Native American jewelry. The movie theater is called The Opera House. When it opened in 1910, charging 5¢ for a moving picture show, it took pride in delivering "wholesale entertainment for the masses at a moderate cost."

You can try the new cappucino bar, or, if you're after an older atmosphere, try the Mecklenberg Inn, a 1793 tavern that serves drinks from its wooden bar and looks like a British pub. On weekends the Tudor Hall Farmer's Market, just off German Street, offers fruit and produce, potted chrysanthemums, and wreaths of dried flowers.

The Yellow Brick Bank is where you want to eat. The bank was auctioned off in 1976 and the vault stands open and in use as a wine cellar, while the teller cages have been converted into dining space. It's airy and cheerful, with clouds painted on the ceiling and a ficus tree with fake apples tied to the branches. The waiters and waitresses are young and enthusiastic and, for some reason, wear what look like lab coats.

After lunch you might want to take a look at O'Hurley's General Store. Everything you didn't know you wanted can be had here for a fair price from Jay O'Hurley, who was born upstairs but had to wander around a bit before it became clear to him that you can't take the country out of the boy. Horse harnesses, handcarved, wooden pitchforks, toys made by West Virginia whittlers, quilts, washboards, fiddles, clocks, guns, stoves, and jeans, are, as he says, "commonly available." You expect to see a horse and wagon waiting patiently outside, and probably you do sometimes. You could be in a time warp.

For accommodations there is the Bavarian Inn where you'll likely sleep in a four-poster bed in one of the chalets with a view. If you prefer a bed and breakfast, try the Thomas Shepherd Inn, a 125-year old home on land originally owned by the town's founder, furnished with post-Civil War antiques and run with enthusiasm and warmth by innkeeper Margaret Perry. For weekenders, the Antietam Battlefield is a few miles away.

CHARLES TOWN

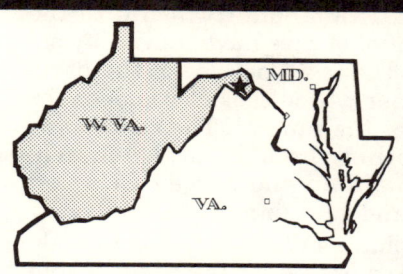

For a day at the races, Saratoga is more fashionable. For a quick trip to the $2 window, Laurel is closer. But at Charles Town, West Virginia, the nags run with a backdrop of hazy blue mountains, and the road that leads there is a pastoral adventure through green fields edged with honeysuckle-draped fences and dotted with mimosa trees. Just an hour and a half from downtown Washington you are in deep country where cows go wading in clear streams and hawks circle overhead. And 30 minutes after the last race you can slip into a rocking chair on the porch of a bed and breakfast in Harpers Ferry or Shepherdstown. More I cannot wish you.

Of course, it's true that the Charles Town Races, Inc., thinks of a hundred ways to separate you from your money, which you could easily accomplish all by yourself at the betting windows. There's the admission charge and the cover charge and the drinks and the charge for the very chair you sit on. And then, of course, you must have the Racing Form and the program and a tip sheet, or how are you to know where to lose your money? But then the bugle sounds and they're off and rounding the turn, and so what if you're collecting a string of unredeemable tickets? Luck might turn in the next race so, meanwhile, watch my binoculars while I lay out another $2.

You can eat quite decent Maryland crab in the air-conditioned club dining room and keep an eye on the horses from the table. The view's good from nearly every vantage point and everybody stands up for the finish anyway. Put the meal on the credit card and save the cash for the horses. Post time Friday and Saturday is 7:15 P.M., and on Sunday, 1:30.

But there's more to Charles Town (pop. 3,122) than the horses. This is the town laid out by George Washington's youngest brother, Charles, and here the Washingtons lived for many years. Quite a few of them lie in the graveyard of Zion Episcopal Church, mingling their bones with the Confederate soldiers who came later. The church itself was built in 1852, and is worth getting off the main street to look at.

A great-great-grandson of Thomas Jefferson lies here, as well as a grandson of Edmund Randolf, first secretary of state. Many collateral descendants of George Washington are buried in the churchyard, more than 20 all together born on his estate in Mount Vernon.

Zion Episcopal has been inextricably intertwined with the town since the beginning and a lot of stories have inevitably accumulated about its early days. There is the tale of the early funeral of a well-known parishioner whose casket was open for viewing in his home all day before the funeral. The casket was sealed that night and in the morning brought to the church, where late arriving relatives showed up and begged for a last look. Their request was granted, and out jumped the family cat.

Happy Retreat, the home of Charles Washington on Blakely Place, is in private hands, and Claymont Court, the beautiful old home Bushrod Washington (a great-nephew of George) built in 1820, is now a school. Although Claymont Court is no longer open to the public, you can drive by, and you may even see someone who could take you through. To get there, take Route 13 nearly 6 miles out of Charles Town toward Summit Point. You will see a sign for Claymont Court; drive back into a wooded area and look for it on your left.

It was at the Jefferson County Courthouse, corner of North George and East Washington Streets, that John Brown, the Harpers Ferry abolitionist, was tried for treason. It's a nice old 1836 red brick building that was rebuilt after the Civil War shelling it sustained and now is open to the public from 9 A.M. to 5 P.M. Monday through Thursday and until 7 P.M. Friday. The original courtroom where Brown was sentenced survived undamaged, and a few mementos, including a wagon of Brown's, are on display. At the corner of South Samuel and Hunter Streets you can see three stones taken from his jail cell, which now mark the spot where he was hung. Troops under the command of Stonewall Jackson were drawn up at the base of the scaffold.

Other points of interest are the Free Black Schoolhouse and the old Opera House. The schoolhouse, at the intersection of Summit Point and Middleway Roads, next to the Baptist church, was built when the Charles Town District Board of Education bought the lot in 1867 for $100 and commissioned construction of the town's first free black schoolhouse. Before that, classes for black children were held in a house on Liberty Street.

The old Opera House, at the northwest corner of George and Liberty Streets, was commissioned by a Washington family descendant and built in 1912. It has an orchestra pit, curved balcony, and seats 290 people. The building was abandoned from 1948 to 1973, but now it holds live theater performances.

(The most recent season had everything from "Oliver!" to "To Kill a Mockingbird.") Call (304) 725-4420 for a schedule.

If you want to eat right in Charles Town, try the Charles Washington Inn on Liberty Street. Otherwise, it's not a far drive to Shepherdstown or Harpers Ferry.

The Jefferson County Chamber of Commerce has up-to-date information on this old town; call (304) 725-2055 or (800) 624-0577. Ask for the "Bicentennial Guide to 'Old' Charles Town, 1786-1986," which maps out a walking tour.

BERKELEY SPRINGS

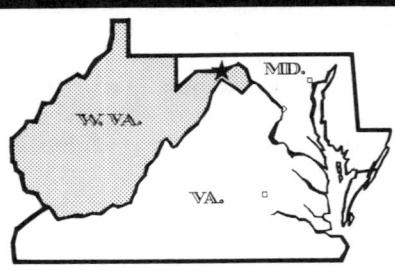

The fashionable have moved on from Berkeley Springs. The big old wooden hotels that could house 500 guests seeking relief from arthritis, gout, high blood pressure, or nerves have mostly burned to the ground. The clear, warm waters still gush from the steep ridge as they did when George Washington lowered himself into them back in 1748. But the Pullmans that once brought the crowds from Philadelphia and New York are gone, and the town is now just a small village sleeping in the West Virginia sunshine.

No matter. In fact, all to the good. This is a wonderful village, an anachronism that will charm you. It has everything—a nice country inn, a view that will make you catch your breath, a romantic castle, a movie house with overstuffed chairs for box seats (25 cents extra), and of course, the baths.

Berkeley Springs, I love you.

Right off the bat, you're in a good mood because the drive to wild, wonderful West Virginia is pretty. West (by God) Virginia (as the natives call it) has some of the last really unsullied-by-development scenery in this part of the country. Two or three miles beyond Berkeley Springs on Route 9W is an overlook from which you can see the Potomac River winding its way through three states, a view rated by the National Geographic Society (according to a nearby marker) as one of the most beautiful in the country.

And then there's the Country Inn. Jack Barker and his wife Alice run this inn in a way that makes you feel cherished. When he first took it over years ago, it was an old ladies' home. Now, there's dancing to top 40 tunes on Saturday night in a lovely garden where one of the inn's buildings has been built around some trees. The Country Inn is furnished with antiques and has a nice old-fashioned feel to it. In keeping with what Berkeley Springs is famous for, the inn has made a modern addition, the Renaissance Spa, where you can partake of whirlpool mineral baths, massages, facials, manicures, and pedicures in a crystal and chrome setting. The inn and spa are at (800) 822-6630.

Berkeley Springs is a village of less than 800 people. It's largely a one-street affair and holds events like apple butter festivals and reunions for the high school class of 1950. Georgetown it is not, and it sneaks up on you. You can talk to the people you meet and they don't look on you as a tourist. It seems to have a slightly schizophrenic difficulty with its name. Officially it is the town of Bath, West Virginia, but the post office calls itself Berkeley Springs.

The thing to do in Berkeley Springs is to take the baths. It's a good idea to make reservations, which you can do up to two weeks in advance by calling (800) CALL-WVA. The baths are open from 10 A.M. to 4:30 P.M. every day except Christmas and New Year's. You can get a massage, too, for $30, or just a bath for $18.

You can choose from a Roman bath in a sunken pool (good for exercising while you're in it, if you really want to be healthy) or a heat cabinet that surrounds you with vapor steam at a temperature of 124 degrees for 8 minutes. The other baths are heated to a mere 102 degrees. All are private. (This is West Virginia, not California.)

Outside, you can see the natural stone bathtub that George Washington used at the age of 16 when he was surveying with Lord Fairfax in the vicinity. Children gambol in the long canals of the runoff from the springs, and people sit in the park and watch. The National Register of Historic Places has put the baths on its list.

And then there's the castle. Nobody who comes here should miss it, if only to find out about the man after which Suitland, Maryland, was named. It seems a Colonel Suit, age 48, met a 16-year-old girl named Rosa to whom he proposed marriage. He was rejected. Hearing that she sighed for a castle, he promised to build her one if she would reconsider. The offer was too tempting, and they were married. Work on the castle began in 1881 and was finished in 1885, but by that time the colonel was dead.

From there, the story takes on something of a moral tone. For Rosa lived high, wide, and handsome, orchestras playing all night, and her guests stayed on expensively a week or more. What with all this, Rosa had to mortgage the castle and eventually lost it. She got by for a while raising chickens, but at length one of her sons appeared from the west and took her home to live with him. She died there in her 90s. Call (304) 258-3274 to check the hours the castle it is open.

The Country Inn has a rival just outside Berkeley Springs, the mountain retreat of Coolfont, a recreational area hidden in 1,200 acres of wooded land in a valley between Cacapon Mountain and Warm Springs Ridge. If, instead of poking about in small town history, you prefer boating and swimming and organized recreation, you can pay a reasonable price and do these and more at Coolfont. Food with a view is offered in the Treetop

House Restaurant, and there's plenty of planned activity—a monthly "healthy happening," sketching classes, diet regimens, and music on weekends—and it draws the crowd that likes scheduled play. It is handsome, and a great favorite for business meetings and conventions. Call (800) 888-8768 or (304) 258-4500. Berkeley Springs also has several bed and breakfasts; call the Chamber of Commerce, (304) 258-3738, for information.

THE GREENBRIER

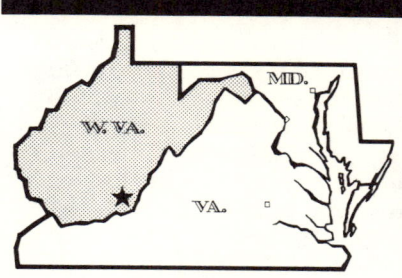

Once in a while it hits you.
Once in a while you feel the need to spend a wad of money, to be cherished as the rich always are cherished, to see what it's like inside the haunts of those who never count their change. Constant budget watching can be soul shriveling—for these moments the answer could be West Virginia's resort, The Greenbrier, a posh watering hole that ranks with the top. The Greenbrier is the main reason cars turn west off Route 81, across the Alleghenies into the Mountain State, summer or winter, bearing vacationers who crave elegance showcased in a magnificent mountain setting.

The Greenbrier has few equals. Like an ocean liner, it assumes complete responsibility for its guests, offering them everything from skeet shooting to tea in the lobby with a violin and piano duo playing in the background. On its 6,500 acres in the Allegheny Mountains, its motto, "Ladies and gentlemen served by ladies and gentlemen," seems like an alluring anachronism after a week of office politics and working late. It would be almost enough if all you did was gaze at the scenery, which is spectacular.

Though most of the Greenbrier's guests never leave the preserve, a little exploring in the nearby towns of Lewisburg and Hillsboro make a country adventure that is a refreshing antidote to unadulterated luxury. Look a little farther and you see something of the real West Virginia.

But first, the Greenbrier.

Sixteen hundred employees work tirelessly to please the visitors. They stand ready to sharpen their golf game, work on their tennis backhand, immerse them in mineral baths, manicure the grounds on which they stroll, and generally shine up the old establishment. If the price tag for all this is stiff, few things in life are free and the visitors are largely well heeled.

"The spot has the first and most important elements of a summer resort—remoteness from cities, landscape and architectural beauty and a delicious atmosphere," wrote John Cooke back in 1878 in *Harper's New Monthly Magazine*. By that time the miraculous cure of Amanda Anderson, nearly incapacitated by rheumatism but dramatically relieved in the spa spring waters, was an old story. Mrs. Anderson, who arrived on a litter, had to be lowered into the waters but jumped from the springs under her own power shouting, "I'm cured, I'm cured!" The reputation of the springs was made.

The first guests of the spa were southern and the Greenbrier is southern in its atmosphere still. "It's sleepy time down south," says the sign in the corridor warning late revelers not to disturb those who have already retired. General Robert E. Lee favored the spa in its earlier incarnation as the Old White, and belles of the South flocked here looking for suitable husbands. But in 1910 the C&O Railroad bought the resort, and soon the private railroad cars of northern moguls lay on the White Sulphur sidings. The Astors and the Vanderbilts found they too liked the Greenbrier.

Amtrak still comes down from Washington three times a week, pausing in White Sulphur Springs—by special request, naturally. The private cars are gone, but memories linger. When the C&O hired Dorothy Draper to give the old resort a new image after it had served as a hospital during World War II, she concocted an eye-catching splash of primary colors with huge areas of white as a foil. Looking at the finished product with satisfaction, she worried about the railroads. "I don't want any smoke-belching engines to come within 5 miles of my new white hotel," she said. Inasmuch as her employer was the C&O, hers was not the last word on the subject.

Maybe to suit the grandeur of the mountains surrounding it, the Greenbrier's scale is massive. The ceilings are grandly lofty; the corridors of the 650-room building are long; 40 miles of carpet cover the floor. Dorothy Draper's wallpaper roses are as big as cabbages. You could roast an ox in most of the fireplaces. But then, a small country inn here would look like the house of a gnome with Kate's Mountain looming over it.

Some resorts that can remember the Civil War might take on a dowager image, but not the Greenbrier. Everything looks sharp here in White Sulphur Springs and even the carriage horses are given extra rations to keep them sleek. Fresh flowers are everywhere, whisked away the moment they are past their prime.

The resort goes through periodic renovations to keep things looking up to date. The spa was recently redone, and now it offers 18 treatments and boasts of being one of the few American spas to follow the European method of using fresh, natural mineral waters, with everything from Swiss showers to aromatherapy and herbal body wraps. This resort isn't just for self-indulgence; you can use all sorts of exercise equipment, receive personal nutrition counseling, or meet with specialists at the Greenbrier Clinic.

The Greenbrier is famous for its three golf courses. Sam Snead claimed he played his best round of golf ever on a course here in 1959, setting a PGA record when he shot a 59 in the third round. The newest course was designed by Jack Nicklaus in 1977.

By the time you've enjoyed the amenities of the Greenbrier, you may agree with this poem, published in a Richmond newspaper in 1833, even though it was referring only to the wonders of the sulphur water:

> Come all you, who thirst for the waters of life,
> Whether father or son, fair daughter, or wife;
> Come, drink at this fount, and you'll certainly find
> Relief for the body as well as the mind.

But it would be too bad to make the Greenbrier your only focus in this handsome country. You should steal away for a while and take a look at the nearby towns and the home of writer Pearl Buck, perched on a mountain some 30 miles away at Hillsboro, a village of 188 people.

The road itself is an adventure. It climbs like a mountain goat path from the center of Lewisburg and offers spectacular views at every turn. Droop Mountain, which you climb, is 3,000 feet high; the route curves like a roller coaster, projecting you into a balcony seat over the valley. You catch your breath again and again.

Pearl Buck's house is white clapboard, with some of the original Victorian furniture inside. The kitchen table is laid for breakfast and the bookcases are full. The winner of both the Pulitzer and Nobel prizes was born here in 1892 and her home is now on the National Register. It is open daily from May through October; for information, call (304) 653-4430.

At the foot of the hill on the way back is a discovery few people know about, The General Lewis Inn, (304) 645-2600, in Lewisburg, chartered in 1782 and one of the oldest towns in West Virginia (when it was founded, the town was in Virginia). The inn is named after General Andrew Lewis, who assembled frontier militia here in 1774 to defeat the Shawnees in an epic battle.

The front desk of The General Lewis Inn once knew the hand of Patrick Henry and Thomas Jefferson. Both registered at this pine and walnut desk about 1760 when it stood in the Sweet Chalybeate Springs Hotel in Virginia. The old stagecoach outside rattled between the springs on the James River and Kanawha Turnpike before it came to rest under the trellis outside the front door.

The inn's fireplaces have the original mantels and everywhere are antiques collected from the three surrounding counties. The hand-hewn beams above your head were lifted from the slave quarters in the rear.

When you see Lewisburg, you're not surprised the old part of town is a National Register Historic District. The nice old 18th and 19th century houses stand flush with the streets, still narrow as they were when this was a way station on the Kanawha Turnpike. The old stone Presbyterian church was built not long after the Revolution, and the Greenbrier County Courthouse, possessor of an unusual cupola, was built in 1837. The Confederate cemetery holds the flower of the South who fell nearby. You can pick up a self-guided walking tour at the inn or ask the visitors center, (304) 645-1000, to send you one.

The food served in the inn dining room is truly southern —pork chops, Virginia ham, homemade soups, and biscuits. It's all as comfortable as an old glove, and the perfect foil for the fleshpots of the Greenbrier.

WILDERNESS RAILROAD

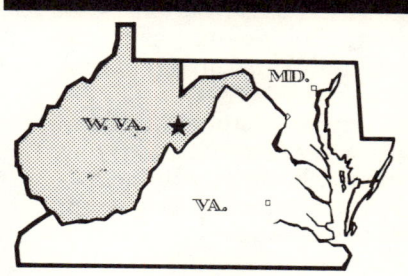

"Dear Sirs," wrote a Cheat, West Virginia, postman to Washington, D.C., headquarters during a winter in which he had delivered no mail for 3 months. "If the gable end of hell should blow out and shower fire, smoke, and melted lava for 40 days and nights, it would not melt the snow enough on Cheat Mountain so as to get your damned mail out on time." He wrote in the 1880s, but nothing has changed much since. That's Cheat Mountain in the winter.

Ah, but in the spring and summer, Cheat is dotted with trillium, bloodroot, and trailing arbutus, and populated with gray fox, mink, bear, and occasional panther and moose—a mountain smiling and handsome as a picture postcard.

To see all this—and the remnants of a ghost town and abandoned sawmill—you don't even have to climb Cheat. Just buy a ticket on West Virginia's old logging railroad at Cass, sit back, and let the landscape drift by at 5 mph. As an antidote to concrete throughways, it has no peer.

West Virginia is one of the country's last unspoiled landscapes—a shunpiker's dream where country roads wind past sheep pastures en route to places called Pipestem, Cutlips, and Droop. Take the historic Staunton-Parkersburg turnpike, Route 250, which still follows the roadbed that a French exile from Napoleon's army laid out to link Virginia with the Ohio Valley, and you will be transported into another era. It's a two-lane highway with nothing between you and the view but an occasional rail fence. Once you're across the border, unless it's a weekend, you may not meet another car for half an hour at a time.

This is wicked country for motorists in winter; it can be snowing a blizzard high in the Monongahela National Forest while back in Staunton, an hour away, it is shirtsleeve weather. These are the West Virginia mountains, which tower nearly 5,000 feet over picturesque valleys, and in spring they are a glory of rhododendron, the state flower. Watch the road curves, though; this is the same roadbed the original engineer laid out.

Cheat Mountain lies a few miles south of Bartow, where you leave 250 for Route 28. The train depot huddles in Cass, an old lumbering settlement surviving from the time the loggers came down from the north to cut the timber on the mountain top. Cass consists of a general store, the depot, and a handful of houses (pop. 148). It looks as if the loggers had just left.

West Virginia once boasted 3,000 logging railroad lines, but the 11 miles of the Cass Scenic are all that survived. The state has equipped the line with old Shay engines, geared steam locomotives that push and pull several open-air cars converted from lumber flatcars to the top of Cheat and Bald Knob, 4,500 feet above the valley. From Memorial Day to October, it hauls tourists up to what naturalists call a piece of Canada gone astray, rising straight up out of the mid-Atlantic terrain below.

The trip to the top and back takes 4½ leisurely hours, and no ocean voyage makes close friends of strangers so quickly. Maybe it has something to do with the nostalgic sound of the locomotive whistle—the lonesome moan out of the past—that creates the ambience. Maybe it's the brakeman on every car, spinning his tales of how it used to be, keeping a weather eye on the brakes on the stiffest grades.

Or maybe it's just that in a speed-happy world, we are easily enchanted with an old time, slow-paced trip like this where we don't have to worry or hurry and have time to smell the flowers.

Standing at the window you can lean out and touch the foliage, watch the world turn gradually from sunny mid-Atlantic to shadowy Canadian wilderness. Many inhabitants of these woods would be at home in Newfoundland or Alaska. Mile by mile the cardinals and Carolina wrens disappear, giving way to birds of cooler climes like rose-breasted grosbeaks and winter wrens. In the spruce forest here dwell mink whose coats are indistinguishable from those in Labrador. Snowshoe rabbits are plentiful. It's a land that scarcely knows summer.

If you're standing by the brakeman, you may see him point out bear tracks, or maybe those of a mountain lion trailing a rabbit. Lean out the window and smell that rarest of all perfumes, the smell of unpeopled, unmanaged, virgin second-growth forest. It's a paradise for people who want nature adventures without the strain of backpacking.

Those who take this trip leave part of their reserve behind. In each car there are always men wearing the railroad engineer caps sold at the store below. Strangers share blankets against the gathering chill as the train climbs, and have been known to exchange sandwiches from their picnic baskets.

The train pushes its way through a nostalgic page of history that began with the turn of the century and the discovery of a valuable stand of red spruce on Cheat. Imported Italian labor drove the ribbons of steel up to the top and men working 11 hours a day cut the timber to make a path. From Canada and the northern states came the lumberjacks whom Cass called wood hicks and who made Cass a miniature frontier boomtown.

Wearing their special shoes and notched hats, they descended on the town from time to time with 6 months' pay in their pockets. In 2 weeks they had spent it all on liquor and a good time and disappeared to get the wherewithal to do it all over again.

A commentator narrates over the public address system, but it is a brakeman who spins the real stories. Like the time a woman lost her poodle over the side of the train and the engineer had to stop while everyone gave chase. The brakemen know the name of every tree and creek and can point out the one-sided, windblown shape of the spruce, the old locomotive stacks left to rust in the valley, and the corpses of trees still standing that were injured in the 1890s by the log slides.

After the trip into the woods, Cass looks like a metropolis. Even so, civilization has not exactly poured over lovely Route 28, and the flavor of West Virginia is still mainly indigenous at Cass. In the country store where you buy your lunch or coffee afterward, navy beans and cornbread cost less than a pack of cigarettes and the music coming out of the jukebox is deep country. The store is the same one that was there when the railroad began.

The train begins the 11-mile trip at noon every day except Monday. And three times daily, at 11 A.M., 1 P.M., and 3 P.M., another train makes a 4-mile run a little less than halfway up. After Labor Day the train runs weekends only, except for the first two weeks in October when it runs Thursday through Sunday to give patrons a look at the foliage. It shuts down for the winter on November 1.

If you have to wait, visit the Cass Historical Museum, stuffed with memorabilia of West Virginia's early logging days, like the bicycle the local doctor used to get to the logging camp. There's also a Wildlife Museum and the Cass Showcase, which has a short audiovisual history of Cass and a model of the town and the trains you will be taking.

This trip is definitely a weekend rather than a day trip from Washington, but there's no need to worry about where to stay. The Cass Scenic Railroad State Park has restored the two-story houses the West Virginia Pulp and Paper Company built for its employees in the 1920s. Each cottage has a fully equipped kitchen and sleeps up to eight people. "Everything but your groceries and personal belongings is provided," the brochure says cheerily. Of course, that doesn't include TV, air conditioner, or phone—but after all, you're on vacation. There's a public phone (very public) on the porch of the Country Store. If you don't want to do your own cooking, there's always the Cass Last Run Restaurant in the Country Store, but remember, you're not in the city anymore: It closes at 6 P.M.

For information on Cass Scenic Railroad, (800) CALL-WVA.

INDEX

Amos, Dr. Walter S. 34
Annapolis 102
Anne Arundel 43
Antietam Battlefield 140
Ash Lawn 47
Assateague 62, 123
—Oyster Museum 63
—Ponies 62
Atlantic Hotel 122

B

B&O Railroad Museum 74
Bankhead, Tallulah 109
Bath 145
Battle Creek Cypress Swamp 130
Bavarian Inn 138
Bealeton Flying Circus 12
Belle Grove 20
Bellevue 117
Berkeley Plantation 53
Berkeley Springs 144
Berlin 119
Berrywine Plantations 84
Betterton 110
Black History 24, 56
Blackwater Wildlike Refuge 115
Booth, John Wilkes 96
Breckenridge, General John 39
Brown, John 132, 142
Buck, Pearl 149
Byrd Visitors Center 33
Byrd, William III 52

C

C&O Railroad 147
Calvert Cliffs 128
Calvert County Marine Museum 128
Cambridge 115
Captain Thomas 41, 68
Carroll, Charles 74
Carroll County 88
—Farm Museum 90
Carter, Charles 51
Carter, George 18
Carter's Grove 58
Cass 151
—Scenic Railroad 152
—Historical Museum 153
Casselman Bridge 94
Charles County 96
Charles Town 141
Charlottesville 45
Chase Lloyd House 104

Cheat Mountain 150
Chesapeake House 66
Chestertown 107
Chincoteague 61
Chinn, Joseph 8
Cider Mill Farm 77
Claymont Court 140
Coach House Tavern 52
Colonial Williamsburg Foundation 60
Cooley, Ghost of Hettie 22
Coolfont 145
Concord Point Lighthouse 79
Country Inn, The 144
Crisfield 65
Cullins, Richard Edward 25
Customs House 107

D-E

Decoy Museum 78
Deep Creek Lake 92, 95
Dickey Ridge Visitors Center 32
Dove 126
Drum Point Lighthouse 129
Dulany, Ida 6
Early, General Jubal 21
Eastern Neck Wildlife Refuge 110
Easton Waterfowl Festival 111
Ellicott City 74
Emmitsburg 84
Eustis, William Corcoran 19
Evans, Colonel Nathan 10
Evelynton Plantation 54

F-G

Faith Mountain Herbs & Antiques 35
Farfelu Vineyards 28, 30
Fauquier County 11, 37
Flag Ponds Nature Park 130
Frederick 92
Frederick County 85
Fredericksburg 13
—Battlefields 15
Free Black Schoolhouse 142
Fritchie, Barbara 85
Front Royal 31
Garrett County 92
General Jubal Early 19
General Lewis Inn 149
Grantsville 92
Greenbrier 147

H

Hall of Valor 39

Hammond Harwood House 104
Happy Retreat 142
Harford County 71, 78
Harpers Ferry 132
—Black Voices Exhibit 136
—Election Day 134
—John Brown Tour 135
—John Harper House 136
Harrisons 53
—Benjamin 53
—William Henry 53
Havre de Grace 78
Henry, Judith Carter 9
Henry, Patrick 46, 149
Herold, Davey 97
Hillsboro 149
Hill Top house 137
Hite Family 20
Hotel Strasburg 35
Howard County Courthouse 75
Howard County Historical Society 76

I-J-K

Imperial Hotel 107
Ingleside Winery 43
J.C. Lore Oysterhouse 128
Jackson, Andrew 75
Jackson, "Stonewall" 9, 142
James River Plantations 50
Jefferson County Courthouse 142
Jefferson, Thomas 21, 28, 45, 149
Jones, John Paul 102
Julia A. Purnell Museum 120
Kenmore 13
Kent Farm 7
Key, Francis Scott 86, 88, 104

L

Ladew, Harvey 71
Laurel Brigade Inn 18
Lawrence of Arabia 72
Lee, Robert E. 19, 51, 135, 148
Leedstown Resolutions 43
Leesburg 17
—Court Days 17
Lewis, Fielding 13
Lewisburg 149
Lighthouses 79, 117, 129
Lilypons 86
Linden Vineyards 29
Linganore Winecellars 84
Lloyd, Bill 97
Loudoun County 17, 24
—Courthouse 17

—Museum 17
Luray Caverns 36
—Stalactite Organ 38

M

Madison, James 20
Manassas National Battlefield Park 9
Maritime Museum 79, 115, 117
Marsteller, Ann Bailey 10
Maryland Inn 106
Maryland Statehouse 105
Martin, Glenn 110
Mary's Rock Tunnel 32
McClellan, General John 11
Means, Samuel 25
Mellon Estate 7
Mercer, Dr. Hugh 15
Michie Tavern 45
Middleburg 5
—Training Center 6
Middletown 20
Mitchell, R. Madison 78
Monongahela National Forest 150
Monroe, James 45
Monticello 46
Morven Park 18
Mosby, John 5
Mount Olivet Cemetery 86
Mudd, Dr. Samuel A. 98

N-O

Nassawango Iron Furnace 119
National Road 82, 92
Naval Academy, U.S. 102
—Chapel 103
—Museum 104
New Market, Virginia, Battle of 38
New Market, Maryland 82
Nicholson, William "Swish" 109
Norris House 18
Oakencroft Winery 48
Oakley 6
Oatlands 18
Oasis Vineyards 28
Octoberfest 138
O'Hurley's General Store 140
Old Jail Museum 11
Old Rag Mountain 31
Opera House 42
Oxford 11

P-Q

Patapsco Hotel 74
Penn Alps 93
Pink House 26

155

Pocomoke River 119
Pocomoke River Canoe Company 120
Poe, Edgar Allan 49
Pollock, George Greeman 32
Prince Georges County 96
Quakers 24, 27

R
Railroad Station Museum 74
Randolph Estate 7
Rappahannock River 40
Red Fox Inn 8
Remington Farms 110
Rising Sun Tavern 14
Robert Morris Inn 116
Robinson, James 11
Rock Hall 109
Rokeby 7
Rose Hill Manor 86
Rudy Thomas 64
Ruffin, Edwin 53
Rumsey, James 139

S
St. John's College 104
St. Mary's City 125
St. Mary's County 125
St. Michael's 116
Savage River 94
Seton Shrine 84
Shenandoah National Park 31
Shenandoah Vineyards 20, 23
Shepherdsown 138
Sheridan, General Phil 21
Shirley Plantation 50
Shriver Family 88
Skipjacks 117
Skyland 32
Skyline Caverns 34
Skyline Drive 32, 35
Snow Hill 119
Solomons 128
Sotterley 127
Sperryville 35
—Apple Harvest Festival 36
Spruce Forest Artisan Village 93
Staunton, Edwin 25
Stone House 10
Stone House Tea Room 18
Steamboat, First 139
Strasburg 35
—Emporium 35
Strawberry Inn 82
Stuart, J.E.B. 5, 19, 55

Surratt, Mary 97
Surratt's Tavern 96
Surrattsville (Clinton) 96
Susquehanna Lockhouse Museum 79
Susquehanna River 78
Swann, Thomas 18
Sykesville 91

T-U-V
Taney, Roger B. 88
Tangier Island 64
"Taps," Composer 52
Thanksgiving, "First" 52
Thomas Shepherd Inn 140
Thornton Gap 32
Tidewater Inn 111
Tillie the Tug 119
Topiary Garden 71
Tred Avon River 116
Trinity Episcopal Church 6
Tudor Hall Farmer's Market 140
Twain, Mark 137
Union Mills Homestead 88
Uniontown 89
University of Virginia 48
Upperville 5

W
Walsh, Dr. Harry K. 113
Warren Green Hotel 11
Warrenton 11
Washingtons
—Betty 13
—Bushrod 142
—Charles 140
—George 8, 13, 85, 104, 144
—Martha 14
Waterford 24
—Black History Tour 24
—Foundation 26
Waterfowl Festival 111
Wayside Inn 20, 22
Westminster 90
Wheatland 43
Whiskey, Invention of 53
White Sulphur Springs 148
White Swan Tavern 108
Widehall 107
Williamsburg 56
Wm B. Tennison 129
Wilson, Woodrow 137

X-Y-Z
Yellow Brick Bank 140
Zion Episcopal Church 140